THREE NAILS ONE PURPOSE

40 Readings for Following Christ to His Cross and Resurrection

DR. JOHN S. LEWIS

THREE NAILS
ONE PURPOSE

40 Readings for Following Christ to His Cross and Resurrection

First Edition Trade Book, 2017
Copyright © 2024 by Dr. John S. Lewis

Also available by Dr. John S. Lewis:

Finding the Treasure in Christmas: Advent Traditions for Families with Kids of All Ages
The Kingdom Story Experience - Old Testament
The Kingdom Story Experience - New Testament
Discipleship Reframed: Building a Framework for a Culture of Disciple-Making

ISBN: 979-8-9871352-4-2

Editorial: Inspira Literary Solutions, Gig Harbor, WA
Book Design: CarrotStick Marketing, Gig Harbor, WA; Left Corner Design, Tacoma, WA
Cover Design and Editing: inMode, Maple Valley, WA
Printed in the USA by IngramSpark

This book is dedicated to my three children:

Jonathan, Ellie, and Rachel,

that you may come to know this story
as well as you know the Christmas story,
and participate by God's Spirit
in Christ's death and resurrection
here and now in your life journey.

Iknew this writing approach was a hit when I read aloud the narratives on the Last Supper to my intergenerational communion class. All ages were on the edge of their seats, gripped by the conversational perspectives of Judas and John at the Passover table with Jesus. Hearing the events of that night from "them" was far more interesting than hearing from me, the teacher! Year after year, this book will capture your heart and prepare it for the Lenten and Easter seasons.

—**Kami Wright, Director of Children's Ministry, Maple Valley Church**

The author Pat Conroy wrote: "The most powerful words in English are, 'Tell me a story.'" We are, at our core, narrative beings. Humanity's sense of the significant and small, attraction and aversion, the beautiful and banal, all find their meaning in story. John Lewis' set of retellings on the passion story allow the reader to stop and see ancient texts in fresh ways. This is a wonderful resource for the journey of faith.

—**Dave Hillis, Colangelo Carpenter Innovation Center Senior Fellow, Author of *City as Playground***

In this collection of readings, John doesn't explain the meaning of the cross or a theology of atonement. That comes later. Here he invites you to experience and come nearer to the story, scene by scene, character by character, line by line teasing out the passion and purpose of the Cross. The approach makes all the difference.

—**Kris Rocke, Director of Street Psalms, Author of *Geography of Grace and Meal from Below***

What never surprises me, but always satisfies me, is coming across someone or something that has recognized the power of the greatest story ever told in new and fresh ways. In short—and every generation needs to do this—to find the particular drama of our time within this larger story. John Lewis achieves this. Moreover, what is particularly attractive about John's work is that you need to appropriate your feelings, thoughts, imagination, physicality—in a word your humanity—to access it. This is no small feat. It takes great skill and a heart saturated with love for both the text and the person who will eventually pick it up and read it. Having been around a while—an 80+ year old Catholic—I have seen a lot. It is from this vantage point that I highly recommend John's Lenten reflections on the Cross.

—**Dr. Reid Carpenter, Founder and Founder Emeritus of the Global Leadership Foundations Network**

ere is a bright book of meditations designed to take the reader more deeply and prayerfully into the mysterious divine plan rooted in the death and resurrection of Jesus. John offers forty consecutive meditations, each designed according to a similar format that can be followed for forty days or simply one after the other, at whatever pace a reader chooses.

In each meditation, short passages of the gospel texts of the Lord's passion and death are accompanied by reproductions of beautiful paintings chosen from various centuries and different styles. Then the gospel passage and scene is entered by means of an imaginative retelling from the point of view of one of the persons somehow involved. Each retelling reveals the same amazing conclusion: the death of Jesus was no accident but rather the mysterious design of God's loving plan to save the world.

Each reflection ends with a prayer. The prayers that Lewis offers are a model for how to come to the Lord Jesus, expressing our thanks and adoration to him for the enormity of his love and for the communion he gives us in the hidden power of his death and resurrection.

I join John Lewis in inviting others to stand in awe and wonder at the divine beauty embedded in the death of Jesus and manifested in his resurrection. This book invites us all to do that.

—Abbot Jeremy Driscoll, O.S.B. Abbot of Mount Angel Abbey

ACKNOWLEDGMENTS

I am grateful to the rainbow of people who contributed to this book and project. Michelle Gray was the first to touch up and revise the first-person retellings, adding a greater sense of drama to my original vignettes. Her work with me accelerated my desire and courage to move these reflections to a book form. Arlyn Lawrence, Kerry Wade, Jennifer Tabert and Karen Bouchard along the way did what good editors do: they thinned the excess and increased the vibrancy and clarity of the stories. Al and Virginia Abbott and Holly Knoll's work on the design made this book beautiful.

Thanks most of all to the Father for offering his Son, for Jesus' immense love from beginning to end, and for the inspiration of the Holy Spirit that led the gospel writers to share the story of Christ's death in such great detail. In doing so, they left us a lifetime treasure, and a fertile place for Jesus followers to nurture an enduring faith, hope, and love.

Falling in love with the significance of the story of the Cross has been a lifelong journey for me. On this journey, I have been greatly influenced by other authors who have written about Christ's passion with insight and conviction. When I was in college, William Barclay's writings on the historical background of the Bible began to open my mind to many details of the cross story and why they were included in the first place. I was intrigued. That's when God used the writings of Brennan Manning and John Stott to set the hook, for through them and others, I came to believe there is no greater revelation of God's greatness than in the passion story. I realized the cross is not only a doorway to forgiveness, but each of the smaller stories invite me to see myself in them. In Matthew 26-28, I find inspiration and comfort in my own call to carry his cross.

Other authors have instilled in me the confidence and permission to "rewrite the story" with both freedom and caution, with reverence and embellishment. In the preface of her classic *The Man Born to Be King*, Dorothy Sayers provided her rationale for reinterpreting the gospel stories as a play and drama. She contended that it's imperative to retell the old, familiar story in innovative ways for each generation. Her words were the wind in my sails for developing these 40 retellings. Many of Max Lucado's books and Ken Gire's *Moments with the Savior* helped me experience the power of a Bible story well retold.

The experiences of these and other writers and teachers (as well as many others) contributed to my conviction that the story of the Cross and all the biblical stories can be rewritten and retold with great profit for every generation and without anything essential being added or deleted.

Here are my heartfelt wishes for you, myself, and anyone else who takes a walk through these stories, prayers, and reflections of Jesus' Calvary passion and purpose:

- ❖ That our minds reason well, and that our imaginations aid us to enter in as participants.
- ❖ That our souls' emotions find space to be transparent and genuinely expressed.
- ❖ That our wills be prepared to make courageous choices in the struggles that matter most.
- ❖ That God's strength be ours for the next step of taking up our own cross.

In a real world of pain, how could one worship a God who was immune to it? I have entered many Buddhist temples and stood respectfully before the statue of Buddha, his legs crossed, arms folded, eyes closed, the ghost of a smile playing around his mouth, a remote look on his face, detached from the agonies of the world... And in my imagination I have turned back to that lonely, twisted, tortured figure on the cross, nails through hands and feet, back lacerated, limbs wrenched, brow bleeding from thorn-pricks, mouth dry and intolerably thirsty, plunged in God-forsaken darkness...I could never myself believe in God, if it were not for the cross.

– Peter Kreeft

"*ho do you say that I am?*" From the very beginning, there have always been different opinions about Jesus. In his lifetime, some thought he was Elijah reincarnated, others John the Baptist risen from the dead, a good teacher, or a miracle man.

Others who called him "Messiah"—Peter at Caesarea Philippi and the crowds on what we now refer to as Palm Sunday—held deep misconceptions about him. As for the religious leaders, their unbelief was fueled by concerns about maintaining true faith as they understood it, a desire to maintain their privileged (and lucrative) positions, and fear of provoking the Romans.

Of course, ordinary folks who might have believed in him would have been intimidated by the priests. Many presumed that a true Messiah would not suffer shame and torture no matter how many astounding miracles were attributed to him. After the events of Jesus' life and especially his death, only two options were really possible:

The first was that Jesus had simply pretended to be the Messiah and, therefore, received his just due from his Jewish and Roman enemies in death. Unfortunately, after Jesus' death, many people—even those who had followed him—found themselves in this camp. In those days, people believed suffering was a sign of God's curse. Even those who had called Jesus Messiah were confused, convinced that his shame and death on the cross could not be part of a divine plan.

The second possibility was that Jesus was indeed the promised Messiah but radically different from the long-held expectations of the Jewish people.

Matthew Brings the Truth to Light

Inspired by the Holy Spirit, Matthew set out to settle the debate once and for all. He wrote as if he were Jesus' appointed lawyer. And, as if his readers were a jury, he hoped to persuade them with facts and logic.

Like all the gospel writers, he laid out in his passion account a second vantage point, serving as a "cross-examination" of the witnesses. He includes the "prosecuting attorney's" accusations that Jesus was a false prophet and a criminal worthy of his sufferings.

The charges were that Jesus, exposed as a fraud by one of his inner circle, lost control of his subversive plot against Rome. He lied to his followers and received what he deserved as a guilty traitor. And as far as the outrageous claims that Christ rose from the dead, clearly, the disciples stole the body and misled the masses.

Matthew's retelling of the crucifixion and resurrection story confronts these accusations head-on and serves to this day as a defense of Jesus' claims. His account addresses the misperceptions and arguments of Christ's skeptics and opponents, including Jewish zealots, priests, Sanhedrin, Greek philosophers, and religious Gnostics.

Matthew wanted his readers to see that Jesus had been wrongly labeled, that he was not, as they claimed, a dangerous blasphemer, a religious pretender abandoned by his disenchanted disciples, or a tried criminal receiving his just due.

No, Matthew argued, there was a larger story all these others had overlooked. No detail or event of Jesus' last week happened by accident. All were a part of the greatest act of love ever to visit Earth…all part of the Father's eternal and compassionate plan for our salvation.

Matthew's story is not merely biographical but also apologetic, presenting evidence to skeptics that their disbelief in Christ as a suffering and risen Messiah remains unfounded.

Finding Our Story in This Story of Jesus

Matthew's audience was the early Church, beleaguered by persecution, struggle, and shame. The story of the Cross spoke directly to their suffering: "Christ who suffered for you on the cross is the one who is with you now in your suffering. There is purpose in your suffering because there was purpose in his. There is meaning in the places where everything feels absurd."

That's good news for those who hurt or mourn, and it's as meaningful today as it was then.

Matthew intends to do more than persuade the people Christ understood their suffering. He also invites readers, then and now, *to fully surrender our hearts and lives to this same Jesus*. As we read the words of this disciple, the perceived pointlessness of the death of Christ transforms into meaning, into a starting point from which we, too, can begin to interpret our own life and death.

To be human is to encounter suffering. Life disappoints us, and in our struggles, we ask: "What is the purpose of this?" Shame has a way of creeping in and suggesting subtle

lies. Our shoulders begin to sag, and our gaze drops when we focus on half-truths.

Then, the message of Matthew finds a home with us, inspiring us to invite Christ's presence into our own journey of the Cross. As his followers, we, too, in our own limited way, suffer and "die" before we rise in glory—first here on Earth and then after our bodies perish. In fact, the heart of the New Testament message is this: Christ, through his Spirit, seeks to live in us not only his life but also his death and resurrection.

Let it be so in us, and may these pages spur us on to that end!

What This Journey Holds

In the following pages, the account of Jesus' death and resurrection in Matthew has been divided into 40 readings. Each reading includes:

1. An image of a sacred painting reflecting the Matthew passage of the passion story

2. A passage of Scripture from Matthew

3. A "Story Retold," in which you will find an extended paraphrase from the standpoint of one character in the story. These stories elaborate on the historical background we might miss 20 centuries later and details we might overlook in a casual reading. I have sometimes used a "sanctified imagination" to fill in what Matthew's brevity did not allow him to include. These retellings do not replace nor have the same

authority as the Scripture, but they have helped the story come alive for many

4. A short prayer

5. An opportunity to reflect and apply the insights from that day's reading.

Best Ways to Read This Book

I aim to retell the Cross and Easter Story so that you are prepared to appreciate its history and integrate it into your present story.

As you journey through its days and settings, you are invited to identify with different characters and see Jesus with fresh appreciation. Bring your sufferings, struggles, and even your shame again to Christ as you experience this most important of all stories.

The death and resurrection of Jesus is the cornerstone of the truth about Jesus and the basic pattern of following the Master. For example, we must take up our cross daily, die to ourselves, and grow into his life. Every time we take communion and read about the Lord's Supper, the invitation rings out to all of us: "Come, remember Christ has died and risen. Come worship. Come die and rise with him until the Risen Lamb comes again in glory!"

No wonder this story can bear fruit in our lives at any time of year! With that in mind, this devotional has no right or wrong time for reading. Here are some suggestions for getting the most out of this book:

❖ Do the readings during Lent, which encompasses the 40 days before Easter. Let it be an annual tradition for setting your heart's posture for the season.

❖ Enjoy it as a personal devotional and go at your own pace.

❖ Go through the book with a small group at whatever time of year works best for your participants.

Reading During the 40 Days of Lent

❖ Lent starts on Ash Wednesday, so there are four days in the first week and six days per week for the next six weeks. Sundays don't count since they are "Easter days" according to the traditional Church calendar.

❖ Readings 37 - 40 are for those who wish to follow the chronology of the story more closely during Holy Week. You can read these after Good Friday.

As You Begin

As you enter into each day's readings, look carefully at our Lord's passion. *The Passion*, formally stated, is the short final period before the death of Jesus. It means to endure or suffer. Decide for yourself if his purpose is meaningful for you and true.

Jesus asked us all, *"Who do you say that I am?"* My wish for you is to be bathed in love as you encounter the Lamb of God throughout this story and live into that question more deeply.

- John S. Lewis

James Tissot, *The Chief Priests Take Counsel Together*, 1894, Watercolor and Graphite on Paper

A Word from Matthew (26:1-5)

When Jesus had finished saying all these things, he said to his disciples, "As you know, the Passover is two days away-and the Son of Man will be handed over to be crucified." Then the chief priests and the elders of the people assembled in the palace of the high priest, whose name was Caiaphas, and they schemed to arrest Jesus secretly and kill him. "But not during the festival," they said, "or there may be a riot among the people."

Matthew the Disciple Speaks

Before I met Jesus, I was a tax collector. The day the Master saw me, heartless and still cheating others at my money table, he called out my name. Against every convention, he invited himself over to my house for dinner.

I've never been the same since. And I'm not the only one. Anyone who met Jesus--and opened their hearts to the message he shared--was changed forever. No wonder his dramatic death left so many of us shattered and reeling. Two questions haunted us:

Were the events of Jesus' death a surprising and unfortunate tragedy of a good man but apparently not the all-powerful Son of God? Or did Jesus die as the Messiah and Son of God, willing everything to happen as it did?

Allow me to tell you what I observed and came to believe-and then you may decide for yourself.

It was obvious from the enthusiasm on the day Jesus triumphantly entered Jerusalem that the common people were filled with hope that he was their Messiah, the Savior they had long awaited. Jesus' popularity threatened the religious leaders. In addition, they were receiving pressure from the Roman rulers to calm down the people.

The Sanhedrin knew if they arrested Jesus during the Passover, the crowds might find out and protest or riot in the streets, demanding Jesus take power. Such a risk could not be taken.

They decided to control the situation by secretly arresting Jesus after the Passover celebration. By then, realizing Jesus wasn't going to overthrow Rome after all, the crowds would become disillusioned and head home. Jesus could be arrested at this point, tried and be rid of once and for all.

During the last week of Jesus' life on earth, he disappointed the crowds. He didn't overthrow the Romans and set up his kingdom as they hoped. Instead, Jesus entered the city of Jerusalem on a donkey, taught in the temple, and did little more than turn over tables of the money-changers.

In other words, he made choices all week that fit his Father's plan for him to die for his wayward people. Even us, his own disciples were under the spell of wanting a victorious Messiah. A crucified Messiah was unthinkable.

In a way, it is strange that we were so unprepared, because Jesus himself spoke of his pending death long before it happened. In fact, in the week before his death, this is what he told us:

"Brothers, as the Passover celebration begins, please be aware of your misunderstandings about the Messiah and God's kingdom. Recall my repeated and past predictions as we walked between the villages: 'I must die at the hands of the religious leaders, then I will be raised from the dead.' Friends, the time for my death is now. Be alert. I know the exact schemes of my enemies and they are playing into a divine and master plan. Don't miss this: it's the Father who is handing me over to their evil intent."

You see, I now believe that nothing happened in the days leading to Jesus' arrest and crucifixion that was a surprise to our Savior.

Unfortunately, by the time Passover week was over, many people thought otherwise. They assumed Jesus' death proved he could not be the Jewish Messiah or Son of God. Sure, he may have done miracles and taught God's law, but when the crucial time came, he failed to show his true colors. People resigned themselves to the reality that the priests rightly determined Jesus guilty of blasphemy, and that Rome justifiably rid itself of a lunatic or potential rival to Caesar's rule.

So I invite you now to come, listen, and decide for yourself what happened though the testimonies of those who were there and share their sometimes-startling conclusions.

A Prayer for the Heart

Father, open my eyes and ears as I read the greatest of all stories—how and why your Son died on the cross and rose from the grave. Was his suffering on Calvary an accident or the result of your initiation? The verdict matters to us all, especially those who have faced chaotic, difficult times since I have also wondered if my chaotic world has a purpose. Guide me toward your truth, and then help me live into your Son's death and resurrection.

Reflect

How did Jesus' death and resurrection first become meaningful to me? What is one hope I have as I begin this book's immersion into the story of the Cross?

Peter Rubens, *Feast in the House of Simon the Pharisee*, 1620, Oil on Canvas

A Word from Matthew (26:6-13)

While Jesus was in Bethany in the home of Simon the Leper, a woman came to him with an alabaster jar of costly perfume, which she poured on his head as he was reclining at the table. When the disciples saw this, they were indignant. "Why this waste?" they asked. "This perfume could have been sold at a high price and the money given to the poor." Aware of this, Jesus said to them, "Why are you bothering this woman? She has done a beautiful thing to me. The poor you will always have with you, but you will not always have me. When she poured this perfume on my body, she did it to prepare me for burial. Truly I tell you, wherever this gospel is preached throughout the world, what she has done will also be told, in memory of her."

John the Disciple Speaks

I remember well the night we gathered for a meal with friends in Bethany, a village suburb near Jerusalem. We didn't know it yet, but this was the last week of Jesus' life. We still felt the afterglow from Lazarus' resurrection and the Sunday festivities. Our host was Simon, the former leper, now restored by Jesus. The witness of his newfound life brightened the room.

Ever since Jesus' dramatic entrance into Jerusalem, we twelve had joined the Passover multitudes in anticipating what miracles Jesus might do and what salvation he might bring. It was to be a grand week ahead! But what happened at dinner that night showed us how little we really knew.

I remember the timid knock. Everyone stopped talking. Simon went to the door and welcomed Mary inside. She walked straight to Jesus. In her left hand, she gripped a costly perfume in a thin-necked alabaster jar. Of course, she had much for which to be grateful. Jesus had changed her heart and welcomed her as a new student; just this week he raised her brother from the dead!

She stood at Jesus' side, opened the perfume and, without diluting it, poured the entire bottle's contents on his head. We were all taken aback by her extravagant, even wasteful, act.

You should know that in our culture, leaders are anointed with oil as a sign of God's favor and the receiving of a divine purpose. Jesus' baptism in the Jordan river was just this: the Holy Spirit coming as a sign of the Father's love, empowering our master to begin his messianic ministry. What none of us saw that night was the fact that her anointing of Jesus with perfume coupled perfectly with his baptism. The anointing and tears pointed to God's favor on Jesus' impending death, to a day when his mercy and Spirit would transform us forever.

But, as I mentioned, most of us in that room didn't understand any of this. Rather, we sat there stunned, mouths open, frustrated. A whole year of wages had been lost in this single moment of unabashed passion.

Other people who wanted to show their support of Jesus had sold items of value and given us the money. Why couldn't she have used a few drops of the perfume to anoint Jesus, then sold the rest and given us the money for the overpriced Passover provisions?

Why was Jesus just allowing this to happen?

Judas was our spokesperson and made the heart of his question appear unselfish: "Jesus, couldn't this perfume have been better used for helping the poor?" As always, the Master rightly perceived our hearts and the core of the issue. Why, Jesus asked us all, were we challenging the woman's loving deed?

Sure enough, our petty selfishness kept us from seeing the deeper meaning of her spilled perfume and overflowing love. Certainly, God's people should care for the poor, but now I can see the crucial lesson we needed to learn that night: it is Jesus alone, not our money or our mission, who deserves our heart's first devotion. The woman understood this much better than those closest to him.

There is one last layer of meaning here. Normally, we Hebrews put perfumes and spices on a body after death. However, Jesus promised us that this woman's anointing before his death would stand as a lasting symbol. Without knowing it, she was preparing Jesus' body for burial. Jesus saw every event through this singular lens of his Father's plan for redeeming the world through his son.

As surprising as this act was, we would later see that Jesus' death would far outdo the extravagance of this grateful woman. No wonder her story will be, as promised, retold in the years and centuries ahead. May future generations read her story and his story, come to worship Christ, and believe that his death was indeed no accident.

A Prayer for the Heart

Thank you, Jesus, for welcoming this woman who, without knowing it, helped me see the incredible cost and purpose of your suffering and death. You, too, would only be understood or appreciated well after your offering of love was given. The pouring of your love and life upon the world far surpassed this woman's kindness. So why do I, like the disciples, sometimes become cynical or worried when your provision is not apparent? Jesus, if I had a bottle of costly perfume and had little else, I believe I would do just what the woman did, right in the face of logic and efficiency. Help my unbelief.

Reflect

How does the woman's extravagance or the disciples' stinginess speak to my devotion to Jesus in this current season of my life?

4

Barna da Siena, *The Pact of Judas*, c. 1350, Fresco

A Word from Matthew (26:14-16)

Then one of the Twelve—the one called Judas Iscariot—went to the chief priests and asked, "What are you willing to give me if I deliver him over to you?" So they counted out for him thirty pieces of silver. From then on Judas watched for an opportunity to hand him over.

Judas the Disciple Speaks

hat a *waste* indeed," I thought as I left Simon's house. As acting treasurer for the group, I felt the pinch of trying to keep a strict budget more than all the others. When Jesus did not stop the woman's reckless waste of perfume, it confirmed my speculations. The Rabbi's passivity extended far beyond this act. I, for one, intended the week ahead to be one marked by action.

If Jesus were truly the Messiah, this week was the ideal time for his full unveiling and the overthrow of our enemies. I was hardly alone in believing that the Passover would be the time and Jerusalem would be the place. We all anxiously awaited the moment Jerusalem would be established as a world center of fame and power. The crowds gathering in the city brimmed with the hope that this would be the pivotal moment for Jesus to unveil his full power upon our Roman oppressors.

But after Sunday, I began to doubt Jesus' timing and approach. He rode into the city on a donkey, suggesting he was to be a path of peace, not power! If Jesus had entered Jerusalem on horseback with trumpets heralding his approach, that would have made his intentions of victory much clearer. It made no sense.

With my confidence now waning, I began to wonder: would Jesus take charge and bring God's kingdom to us, or would he just sit by and let the events unfold without intervening?

My vulnerability to the evil one's lies led me to dismiss Jesus' repeated predictions of his impending death. I began to think I knew better than Jesus what his mission should be.

Here's how my doubts led to my decision to betray my Master: if the chief priests were allowed to find and arrest Jesus, he would be forced to put the coming of his kingdom into motion. What harm would there be in moving up the timetable of what he intended to do all along? Besides, the priests would pay an excellent price to know where he was. The greed that led me to dip occasionally into the money bag gripped me again. I could do a lot with thirty silver pieces.

A few days after the incident with the woman and the perfume, during the bustle of Passover preparation, I slipped out to meet with the chief priests under the guise of running a last-minute errand. My heart was beating quickly, but I didn't let myself think about why.

Making sure I wasn't followed, I wound my way through the crowded streets to the Sanhedrin headquarters. There, I unveiled my scheming plot: "You want Jesus, and I have my reasons to give him over to you. Can we come to an agreement and price?"

From that moment on, I constantly looked for a moment to hand Jesus to the temple guards.

There was something I did not understand then and that so many still do not understand: my self-centered betrayal would be woven seamlessly into Jesus' plan. He would be handed over to his Father's purpose through my miserable scheme.

Incredible.

Even my betrayal, born from my need to control and from Satan's lie, was no accident.

💠 A Prayer for the Heart

God, it's easier for me to be like Judas than I want to admit. Sometimes, you seem quick to wait and slow to act. My words and thoughts often reveal my desire for things to happen on my timetable. You also know all about my own Judas-like distrust and selfishness.

I praise you, sovereign God, for the lesson of this story. While I'm trying to make life work on my terms, you take my sinful attempts and use them for your greater purposes. Lord, I believe that your plans are always better than mine, even if they seem illogical or late to me. Help my unbelief.

Reflect

How might I relate in my own life to Judas' thinking he knew better than Jesus what was best?

The Vaux Passional Manuscript,
The Two Disciples, Peter and John, are Sent to Prepare Passover,
c. 1500, Illustrated Manuscript

A Word from Matthew (26:17-19)

Now on the first day of the Feast of the Unleavened Bread, the disciples came to Jesus, saying to him, "Where do you want us to prepare for you to eat the Passover?" And he said, "Go into the city to a certain man, and say to him, 'The Teacher says, "my time is at hand; I will keep the Passover at your house with my disciples."'" So the disciples did as Jesus had directed them; and they prepared the Passover.

Philip the Disciple Speaks

I wonder how much Jesus actually slept that week between Sunday's fanfare and the Passover. There was something serious and fatigued about the expression on his face, in the way he moved—yet he still used that time to teach and guide us. Now I know the magnitude of what was on his mind, but at the time, I was clueless.

The streets of Jerusalem were teeming with pilgrims and residents making last-minute purchases for the feast. Lambs bleated from nearly every household, soon to play the essential role of sacrifice in the Passover celebration.

Jesus, however, did not seem to share in the cheer of these pre-holiday preparations.

You see, Jesus was a hunted man. The Sanhedrin could no longer ignore this man they deemed a brash impostor, this one who had turned over their temple tables and directly challenged their authority.

With all these things going on, I assumed that the details of the Passover celebration couldn't possibly be on his mind. Naturally, being a detail-oriented, I wondered: *How could all the needed preparations be made if we didn't even know where we would spend the holiday? Where, at this late date, would we find a safe place to celebrate in this overcrowded city?*

I told the other disciples that taking care of these preparations was one way we could help our rabbi. So we approached Jesus and asked, "Where do you want us to prepare the Passover meal for you?"

"As you enter the city," Jesus replied, "you will find a man. Tell him my time has come, and I now need his guest room to celebrate the Passover with my disciples."

Upon hearing these words, we turned to each other with surprise on our faces. Apart from our knowing, Jesus arranged for us to meet a friend of his, the owner of the butcher shop in the city's east market. We had been there on Monday after leaving the temple area. In response to Jesus' inquiry, the man offered his upstairs guest room, far away from the crowds—all we needed to do was let him know when.

It appeared to us that in all the chaos, Jesus was neglecting preparation for a meaningful holiday. In reality, not one small detail of the Passover meal had escaped our Master's planning.

As always, Jesus was one step ahead of us. He again reminded us that he is never caught off guard. He knew all and had arranged all, even in these surprising last hours on earth.

Yes, this would only be the first of many events in the next hours when apparent neglect or chaos would reveal that Jesus was, in fact, perfectly holding the reins of each moment. Even this short and seemingly unimportant addendum to the Passover was no accident.

A Prayer for the Heart

Lord, when my needs seem to go unattended, I can easily doubt that you have prepared the way ahead of me. My doubt reveals that my death-to-self is incomplete and that your death was so necessary.

Jesus, thank you for keeping all things in mind, both things related to your bigger purpose and also my life's most minor details. Everything is in your mighty hand and well-timed unveiling.

Your careful compassion has not overlooked a single detail of my life. I believe you can be trusted in every moment, even when it feels like you've overlooked or forgotten me. Help my unbelief.

Reflect

How can I personally relate to Philip's experience of not noticing Jesus' control over an important detail of my life?

Nikolai Ge, *The Last Supper*, 1866, Oil on Canvas

A Word from Matthew (26:20-25)

When evening came, Jesus was reclining at the table with the twelve. And while they were eating, he said, "Truly I tell you, one of you will betray me." They were very sad and began to say to him one after the other, "Surely you don't mean me, Lord?" Jesus replied, "The one who has dipped his hand into the bowl with me will betray me. The Son of Man will go just as it is written about him. But woe to that man who betrays the Son of Man! It would be better for him if he had not been born." Then Judas, the one who would betray him, said, "Surely you don't mean me, Rabbi?" Jesus answered, "You have said so."

Judas Speaks

Passover Eve had finally arrived. As the sky darkened, we gathered around the table to share the traditional meal that celebrated our liberation from Egyptian slavery. Our past celebrations had been filled with laughter and animated conversation. Tonight, only soft voices filled the room.

As you know, I went to the Sanhedrin just a few days earlier, keeping my scheme hidden from the others. Perhaps that was why it felt especially warm in our upper room, and I was the only one sweating.

Jesus took his place as host at the head of the table. He asked me to sit to his right. I swallowed out of surprise but quickly smiled to acknowledge the unexpected honor. I sat down, my mind scrambling to figure out why he chose me over everyone else.

Soon after we started eating, a shocking statement tumbled from his lips. He said, "I speak to you the truth: one of you will betray me." Now, we all knew there were people out there who sought to betray Jesus; this was the very reason we were hiding here. But our Master was predicting the unthinkable. One from his intimate inner circle of faithful leaders would turn him over to the authorities.

Peter knocked over his cup, spilling wine onto the table. John coughed, choking over a bite of his food. "Surely you don't mean me, Rabbi," each of my co-disciples asked. Each one was simultaneously seeking to declare his innocence, searching his brothers' faces for hints of who might be the betrayer.

Meanwhile, my mind raced. Was Jesus talking about me? If so, how could he possibly have known of my plans? Had someone else seen me sneak away the other night and reported it to him? Trying to look calm, I glanced around, relieved to see that none of their eyes were fixed on me.

Yet Jesus did not seem concerned. His response was cryptic, "My betrayer is the one who has dipped his hand into the bowl with me. What will happen to me has been foretold in Scripture, but woe to my betrayer! He will wish he had never been born." Well, I reasoned, we'd all dipped our hand into his bowl over the years. His clue hardly helped anyone stand out as the betrayer.

I was relieved none of the others seemed suspicious of me. After all, I had deceived myself into thinking I wasn't really betraying Jesus. I was actually helping him. When all was done, I was sure the Master would even thank me, seeing how helpful my plan was for everyone and his kingdom.

Still, I decided it was smart to respond to him like the others had. I turned to him and raised the same question in a lower tone: "Surely not me, Rabbi?"

He turned and whispered, "You have said so."

At that moment it occurred to me that Jesus did know about my Sanhedrin scheme. I interpreted my sitting in the seat of honor as Jesus' affirmation of my plan, a sign that he actually wanted me to be the catalyst for the coming events. I now see differently: sitting at his favored position would protect me from the disciples believing I was the betrayer. All this I missed as I dipped my bread into his bowl.

It was only after the arrest and trial that followed when I was finally honest about my wrong motives. How could I have been so blinded by my own prejudices? Jesus did indeed see everything, including my self-delusion of innocence as well as my greed and heart desire for control. Even though I was a misguided schemer, he let my plans stay their course. He knew my disloyalty was to be woven into his Father's plan for the world's salvation.

Jesus' path of suffering and my betrayal were no accident and no surprise to him. If only I could have understood earlier.

❧ A Prayer for the Heart

Oh Lord, I can hear my heart say, "Surely you don't mean me?" Like Judas, I am often unaware of the extent of my scheming and how I betray your better purposes when I try to take things into my own hands. Yet even when I am blind to your perfect plans and deaf to your words of love and guidance, you give me a place of honor at your table. Jesus, I believe I can love my betrayers and enemies as you have loved me, even if sometimes the enemy is myself. Help my unbelief.

Reflect

How does knowing that Jesus was fully aware of Judas' imminent betrayal speak to me about Christ's character?

Leonardo DaVinci, *The Last Supper*, 1452-1519, Wall Painting

A Word from Matthew (26:26)

While they were eating, Jesus took a loaf of bread, and after blessing it he broke it, gave it to the disciples, and said, "Take, eat, this is my body."

John Speaks

The beauty of ancient song, the scent of roasting lamb and herbs, the reverent hush just before the feast began—even when I was a boy, there was something I deeply loved about Passover. As I grew older and began to understand its rich symbolism, the celebration only became more precious to me.

Every item on the menu helps us remember the story of our people's deliverance from Egypt centuries ago.

The bitter herbs and saltwater represent the many bitter years and tears of our forefathers in slavery. The flat matzah points us to the unleavened bread our ancestors made in haste before leaving Egypt. Lastly, the sweet charoset represents the mud from our hard labor.

And of course, there is the lamb. The roasted meat reminds us of the blood painted on our ancestors' doorposts to avert the spirit of death. Yes, the death of this innocent animal declares the truth that only life sacrificed for life could cover for our sin. Our remembrance of all this is prompted by the host as the meal unfolds and is embellished with hymns and prayers.

All was prepared that night in the upper room for this highly scripted, structured, and symbolic meal. On this particular Passover, however, Jesus would change our beloved liturgy—for good reason and for perpetuity.

As was our custom, he picked up the bread, lifted it up for all to see, and then prayed the usual Passover blessing. But it was Jesus' words of explanation that strayed from the script and caused us to stare long and hard into his eyes. The usual line, "take, eat, this is the bread of the Passover," he replaced with, "take, eat, this is my body, which is broken for you."

I blinked in surprise, looking at the others. Peter was rubbing his chin. Thomas' eyebrows raised. Everyone seemed to be as confused and uncomfortable as I was.

On this side of Jesus' death, I can now grasp his meaning and his invitation: Jesus wanted us to see the divine plan of the horrific hours just ahead. Our Lord made it clear: he was not a zealot planning a revolt, nor plotting a messianic attack on the temple.

Jesus knew that his imminent death was to be his gift to us and his Father. During this, his last earthly celebration, the Master wanted his disciples to know the reason why he would embrace all the suffering of the coming hours.

With the phrase, "This is my body," our Master also declared his death was the fulfillment of the Passover. As Yahweh had used the broken bodies of sacrificed lambs to deliver our ancestors from Egypt, so now Jesus' death would do something even greater.

No wonder John the Baptizer declared at the Jordan river, "Behold the Lamb of God who will take away the sins of the world!" What simpletons we were! He predicted his own death so many times, but our eyes did not see—no, they *would* not see.

I often perceive the deeper meaning in simple truth, but I sure missed it that night. His death on the cross would give us and the whole world a striking new way of relating to our eternal God. And this good news tumbling from Jesus' lips that evening, hidden from the rest of the city, we would soon proclaim to the waiting world.

Beloved, the cross of our rabbi was no accident.

❁ A Prayer for the Heart

God, thank you for this window into the meaning of your death. Thousands of years of longing and waiting culminated in your dramatic table announcement, "This is my body." Father, the Twelve were blessed to hear its arrival, but they did not understand. Amid this world's turmoil and oppression, in my own trials or difficulties in life, it's easy for me to forget your death's many meanings.

Jesus, I embrace the purpose that has come through your suffering and even my own. Take my life, too. Bless it, break it, and give it away, for in doing so, the Passover meal continues, and the world is fed. Help my unbelief.

Reflect

What is one way this reading and prayer helped me better understand Jesus' Last Supper or the meaning of taking communion?

Pascal-Adolphe-Jean Dagnan-Bouveret, *Last Supper*, 1800

A Word from Matthew (26:27-29)

Then Jesus took a cup, and when he had given thanks, he gave it to them, saying, "Drink from it, all of you. This is my blood of the covenant, which is poured out for many for the forgiveness of sins. I tell you, I will not drink from this fruit of the vine from now on until that day when I drink it new with you in my Father's kingdom."

John Speaks

fter Jesus spoke those strange words about the bread broken being like his body, none of us were sure what to think. We whispered between ourselves, wondering what was unfolding before us. I wanted to see the bigger picture, but my mind's eye only held indefinite colors and shapes.

Jesus then suddenly leaned forward and grabbed one of the Passover cups. The next scene was about to begin. In a subdued tone, he spoke the opening prayer. We took hold of our cups, all eyes again fixed on him. What surprising words might come next?

Our Master's words once again strayed from the Passover script: "This is my blood of the covenant, which is poured out for many for the forgiveness of sins."

"Your blood!" I almost exclaimed aloud.

We disciples glanced at each other as we each sipped the cup with Jesus. His words remained for us a total mystery. But now, with so much behind me, I see more clearly: for all those centuries we took the life of spotless animals on the altar, the remedy they offered was only temporary. Jesus spoke of his sacrifice on the cross with this cup.

His death ended centuries of animal sacrifices. It opened the door to what we truly needed--a permanent washing and mercy's lasting peace. Because of this sacrifice, God's new covenant, which our prophets had promised, came to pass at Pentecost. Months later, I'm still rubbing my eyes in disbelief—Yahweh himself now dwells in our hearts and enables us to walk in his ways!

And that's not all.

We would soon be leading others to practice this same new meal. It was as if Jesus were saying to us, "Tonight is the final Passover. In my death, the passing from bondage to freedom and shame to forgiveness will be made possible for everyone forever. You are the first to say 'yes.' Soon, you will be sent to share the same invitation to the world."

After making clear the grand purpose and necessity of his death, Jesus left us a final note of comfort: "I will not drink from this fruit of the vine from now on until that day when I drink it new with you in my Father's kingdom." Not only did our Master predict his resurrection, but he promised a future celebration that death could never end.

Jesus understood us only too well. He could see that the events of his death would leave us confused and despairing. His words may have been disregarded that night, but later...why, even now, these promises of seeing our Lord again make all the difference.

This hope means everything!

To those who were not at the last Passover meal, to those who see Jesus' death as deserved, tragic, and imposed upon him by others, please hear this truth: my Master's cup brings true forgiveness. His death was no accident.

 ## A Prayer for the Heart

Father God, in your Son's bread and wine, we hear your purpose; we witness the divine pattern of a life offered to you. Like the cup, Jesus, you were taken by your Father as a lamb pulled aside for sacrifice. You were poured out in pain, suffering, and death. In all that entailed, you were never abandoned. Instead, you were offered freely as a gift to bless your accusers.

For your love and sacrifice, Lamb of God, I worship you. Holy Spirit, pour out yourself through my life's cup for others. Give me over to those you call me to love and serve. Oh Lord, no matter how many times I slide off your altar, I believe the offering of my everyday life can be a true, holy, and living sacrifice. Help my unbelief.

Reflect

What is one way this reading and prayer helped me better understand Jesus' Last Supper or the meaning of taking communion?

Duccio di Buoninsegna, *The Maesta, 1308, Tempera on Wood*

A Word from Matthew (26:30-35)

When they had sung a hymn, they went out to the Mount of Olives. Then Jesus told them, "This very night you will all fall away on account of me, for it is written: 'I will strike the shepherd, and the sheep of the flock will be scattered.' But after I have risen, I will go ahead of you into Galilee." Peter replied, "Even if all fall away on account of you, I never will." "Truly I tell you," Jesus answered, "this very night, before the rooster crows, you will disown me three times." But Peter declared, "Even if I have to die with you, I will never disown you." And all the other disciples said the same.

Peter the Disciple Speaks

By this time, it was well after sunset. We walked in the night's silence toward the Garden of Gethsemane, a safe place away from the crowds and enemies. Once outside the city walls, we carefully plodded down and then hiked back up the steep, rocky ravine.

The quiet of this night's walk did not match the rancor of my heart. The words of Jesus at the Passover meal hovered over us like a thick cloud. We all quietly wondered what Jesus meant by saying his blood would soon be poured out like wine. And why was our Master so heavy of heart?

If truth be known, I was still upset that I had not sat in the seat of honor at the meal and was confused by his declaration that one of us would betray him. Perhaps the next day's events would not play out as we had hoped.

In the dim moonlight, we stopped. With a steady gaze toward us, Jesus' words came low and sure: "All of you will fall away on account of me."

Still reeling from Jesus' accusation that one of us would betray him, some exclaimed, "No, we won't!" Seemingly unaffected, Jesus continued, "This will happen to fulfill the prophet: 'I will strike the shepherd, and the sheep of the flock will be scattered.'"

By quoting Zechariah, he was trying to show us once again that our falling away would not surprise him, as skeptics would later claim. God's greater story had considered, perhaps even required, our unfaithfulness.

We just couldn't understand this at the time. I believe that is why Jesus spoke his next comforting words: "I will rise from the dead and go ahead of you into Galilee." The Master would first go ahead and then gather his sheep together again. We would not be lost for long.

I blurted out, speaking for us all, "So now you are saying that all of us will abandon and betray you?" As Jesus turned toward me, I added, "Even if all the others fall, I never will!"

Jesus had always loved my confident spirit, but he knew me far better than I knew myself. "I tell you the truth, Peter, this very night, you will do more than flee away. In the few hours that follow, you will deny that you even know me three times."

I couldn't believe my ears! My heart swelled with pride when Jesus first nicknamed me Cephas, the "Rock" on which he would build his worldwide church movement. How could my Master now say that I would crumble in the face of adversity?

How blind I was to my vulnerability!

Desperate to prove myself, I blurted out, "I will die for you before I disown you!" The others nodded in agreement. But Jesus stood his ground. As it turns out, we will see his prediction prove true soon enough.

I didn't know why then, but I understand now that Jesus had to travel this Calvary road alone, wholly set apart from the wayward children he came to rescue.

Skeptics would later interpret my abandonment and denial of Jesus as evidence that he was not the Messiah, much less the Son of God. Ashamed as I still am, I understand now that our weakness fulfilled the Holy Scripture. Our fleeing highlighted Jesus' loyalty to death.

Our unfaithfulness was no accident.

Since then, any future goodness and strength we apostles have demonstrated came from Jesus' mercy and his gift of the Holy Spirit. When the gale winds of fear and misfortune came, only Jesus stayed true.

❤ A Prayer for the Heart

Jesus, the disciples deserted and denied you at your most vulnerable moment—and honestly, I am not that much different, am I? But because you are King over all, even my disloyalty today can be used to highlight your greatness. My heart cries hallelujah at your goodness! God, forgive me for thinking too highly of my human ability to control my behavior and overcome my weakness. The truth is, I can't follow you as I want unless you empower me to do so. Despite our faithlessness, you still call your followers to be your "salt and light" to the world. Amazing! As you did with the first disciples, I believe you will weave even my worst failures into your plan. Help my unbelief.

Reflect

How can I personally relate to Peter's overconfidence in his own strength when life and temptations become difficult?

Sebastiano Ricci, *Prayer in the Garden*, 1730, Oil on Canvas

A Word from Matthew (26:36-39)

Then Jesus came with them to a place called Gethsemane, and said to the disciples, "Sit here while I go and pray over there." And he took with him Peter and the two sons of Zebedee, and he began to be sorrowful and deeply distressed. Then he said to them, "My soul is exceedingly sorrowful, even to death. Stay here and watch with me." He went a little farther and fell on his face, and prayed, saying, "O my Father, if it is possible, let this cup pass from me; nevertheless, not as I will, but as you will."

James The Disciple Speaks

Leaving the city under a canopy of darkness, we arrived at our familiar hideaway, a friend's olive grove. Thick-trunked trees, witnesses to the ages, stood firm in the evening breeze, their branches rustling with their own gentle music. It was oasis-like during the day, but tonight, its refuge felt especially welcome.

Its name, Gethsemane, means "oil press." Olives were squeezed for their oil by placing them under weights of increasing size. Every day, some unspeakable burdens were pressing more and more upon our Lord's heart. Little did we know that out of his excruciating distress, tears would flow, and blood would drip down his brows and cheeks that night.

Just hours earlier, knowing we would desert him, Jesus told us we were his partners and confidants. Here in the garden, at the hour of his great need, came his first request of us.

The Master found Peter, John, and me sitting under one of the trees and whispered, "Please, come close, you three. Surround me like a wall. Lift your hands in prayer like Moses did when Joshua was in battle." Never before had he asked us for such emotional support or encouragement.

How human our Lord revealed himself to be in the garden. Immediately, we left the others to find a nearby place to pray with our beloved Jesus. No longer in sight of our friends, we stood together under the Passover's moon. In its light, evidence of his distress was revealed.

His face was pale and covered with sweat, his eyes red and bloodshot.

For the first time since I met Jesus, I saw fear. "My soul itself aches with sadness," he said, his voice barely above a whisper. "Keep watch, pray for me here while I go over there and pray."

"Of course," we said gently, wanting to comfort him somehow but not understanding what was happening nor knowing how to pray with him.

Leaving us under one of the oldest knotty-tunked trees, Jesus moved farther into the shadows and began to speak to his Father. We could make out only a few of the words as we watched him fall to his knees and press his face to the earth as he prayed.

A little later, Jesus lifted his head and spoke in a voice that easily carried across the grove: "My Father, if it is possible, let this cup of suffering be taken from me. But in the end, this is your plan. Do it your way, for you know best. Here I am. Your will, not mine, be done. I surrender my life into your hands."

I now know Jesus' prayers and sweat poured out in keen awareness of the next day's horrors. Yet even here, carrying his incomprehensible load in the dark night, the Son of God found solid refuge in his Father's will. His garden prayers, like no others, revealed his holiness and humanity.

Our Master's suffering and anxiety, his fear and agony, his blood, sweat, and tears on this night were hidden from the masses. Now revealed to the world, they should not be interpreted as signs of the Father abandoning his Son. The events following his final prayers, which others would soon call chaotic and cursed, were clearly his Father's will.

Jesus embraced the cup of suffering, the cross's unimaginable pain, for the sake of reuniting his Father with his lost children. This intentional offering of his own life has become the hope of humanity.

🜲 A Prayer for the Heart

Lord, You bore the pain of a broken heart. Your garden prayer shows me that you know what it is like to be lonely and to need the comfort of friends. You were tempted to take the easier way but chose the higher and harder road—your Father's cup and Calvary's cross. In Gethsemane's prayer, your human vulnerability coupled well with divine submission. Jesus, my human brother and exalted Lord, help me be honest about my humanity and courageous to pray the same simple prayer, "Not my will, God, but your will be done." Lord, I believe my prayers and life can be more surrendered like yours. Help my unbelief.

Reflect

How might either Jesus' emotions, vulnerability, need for human support, or prayer of surrender, speak to my own story right now?

Giuseppe Cesari, *The Agony in the Garden*, 1598, Oil on Canvas

A Word from Matthew (26:40-41, 43)

Then Jesus came to the disciples after each time he prayed, and found them sleeping, for their eyes were heavy. And he said to Peter, "So, could you not stay awake with me one hour? Stay awake and pray that you may not come into the time of trial; the spirit indeed is willing, but the flesh is weak." And again he came and found them sleeping, for their eyes were heavy.

James Speaks

The night waned on, and our eyes drooped heavy. As Jesus continued to pray, the moon drifted to a new, lower spot in the sky. Not hearing any noise from my other brothers nearby, I stood up and peered through the trees. I spotted a few of our friends stretched out on the ground and could hear some of their familiar snoring and heavy breathing. I saw Peter pacing and yawning repeatedly. Neither John nor I could stop yawning either, as the quiet night enveloped us.

I sat back down and leaned my head against a groove in the rough olive tree trunk. Pale moths fluttered softly in the moonlight. Somewhere in the branches above, a dove cooed, lulling me deeper into the space just before sleep. I pinched my face lightly to try to stay alert, but the effect didn't last long.

My eyes were closed.

The Lion of Judah was here among us, pacing in his Gethsemane cage, pleading with us. "Come with me. Stay with me. Keep watch with me," he implored. I wanted to be there for him, but I didn't foresee how long the honest prayer with his Father would last. None of us understood the tug of war taking place in his heart.

Looking back, Peter, John, and I could have been such a blessing to Jesus if we had remained awake and attentive. Perhaps on an ordinary night we would have risen to the challenge, but not this night. The festivities and confrontations of that week and the late night darkness...well, together they took the upper hand.

His groaning, cries, and prayers continued into the early morning hours, and our best efforts to remain awake fell short. Our eyes slipped from willingness to heaviness to then shutting completely.

Jesus returned, exhausted, and found us every single one of us asleep. I cannot imagine how betrayed and abandoned he must have felt. We especially, as his closest three, had failed him.

All of us knew the Roman policy of putting to death any soldier who fell asleep on night duty. And here we were, a bunch of ragtag young men who lacked even the ability to stay awake a few late night hours for the King of Kings. How could he choose us to be the leaders of his movement someday?

Jesus woke us with a shake on our shoulders and beseeching words that would replay in my imagination for years. "Wake up! Couldn't you resist sleep for even just an hour? Please, stay awake with me," he asked. "Remember, meeting me in prayer will energize your soul with a power greater than your body's weakness or the enemy's temptation. Just because you are willing does not always mean you are able. So tonight, and in the years ahead, imitate me. Pray as I pray, and you will find the power to overcome."

He never ceased to amaze me.

Jesus, even knee-deep in disappointment with this situation, was thinking more of us than himself. He had more than hinted that as leaders of his movement, the future would test our abilities, strength, and character to the limit. Little did we know how crucial our prayer life would soon become.

We needed his rebuke. You would think that this warning would have left all three of us doubly resolute to stay awake. But twice more that night we promised, tried again, and yet still dozed back to sleep!

That night ended up being a life-altering wakeup call. We learned much in our three years with Jesus, but it was apparent we had more learning and growing to do. Much more. For us, even our failure to be his friends turned out to be no accident.

❤ A Prayer for the Heart

Jesus, what a gift it is to see the secret place of your private prayer with your Father. In this dark night of persecution, the early church found both inspiration for its vigilance and grace for its weakness. Lord, I confess that there are so many ways I, too, am tempted to be sleepy, lazy, or distracted from what's most important, even from you. In weakness, lead me to be attentive and meet you heart to heart. When I fall asleep, forgive me; when I choose laziness, rebuke me. Be firm in your mercy and rouse me from my slumber. I believe I can stay alert and pray in a way that makes a difference. Help my unbelief.

Reflect

How does Christ's warning to the disciples, "your spirit is willing but your flesh is weak," speak to my experience of prayer?

Pietro D'Achiardi, *The Agony of Jesus*, 1924, Tile Mosaic

A Word from Matthew (26:42, 44)

Again, Jesus went away for the second time and prayed, "My Father, if this cannot pass unless I drink it, your will be done." So, leaving them again, he went away and prayed for the third time, saying the same words.

James Speaks

y friend Matthew, desiring to be concise, describes Jesus simply praying one short prayer nearly the same way three different times. Jesus' agonizing Gethsemane prayer went on much longer than that. Remember his request, "Stay and pray with me an hour."

Just how long did Jesus pray? To my lingering shame, I cannot remember, for I could not even stay awake for his first round of praying.

As we slept, the moon moved even further across the sky. Of course, for us, the time went on quickly. It seemed but a moment had passed when Jesus woke us from our slumber. But for my Master, the seconds and minutes must have seemed like an eternity. If he had prayed for only an hour, it would have been an agonizing, terrible hour of pacing and crying among the olive trees.

I can imagine Jesus praying that night like the Psalmist of old, "My heart is in anguish within me; the horrors of death assail me. Fear and trembling have overtaken me. Horror has overwhelmed me. Oh that I had the wings of a dove ...I would fly away and be at rest" (Psalms 55:4-6).

In between our failures to stay awake, my brothers and I heard some of what Jesus prayed, and this is what Matthew recorded: "My Father, if this cannot pass unless I drink it, your will be done."

This short prayer revealed the heart of what Jesus prayed that night and what he had lived out all the years I had known him. He found his joy in obeying the Father's will, and did nothing apart from what he was told to do. Thus, when Jesus handed himself over to his arresters, he was actually handing himself over to his Father's leading.

Yet here, in Gethsemane, like nowhere else, we watched Jesus struggle. No joy was his this night to know or do his Father's will.

Have you ever wondered why many future Christ-followers went to their deaths without this same intense struggle beforehand? When Peter was crucified upside down, when Stephen was stoned, when Paul faced certain execution, and when countless others in the early church would give their lives as martyrs, they displayed a level of pre-death serenity we don't see in Gethsemane.

I now see the reason why. It wasn't, as some say, because Jesus was weak. Instead, the death that awaited him was more than the physical pain of a martyr's death. The sin and shame of the whole world would be laid upon his body. Jesus would become our scapegoat--the one prophesied to carry our sorrows and be pierced for our transgressions (Isaiah 53:4-5).

There in the garden, Jesus knew his cross would lead him to experience an agony of heart, a despair of soul, and a death of sin that no other human could bear.

We now see what caused our Lord such distress in his Gethsemane prayer: the anticipation of bearing the world's judgment on his shoulders. The grief and fear our Lord carried into his midnight prayer broke his heart; it even caused the pores of his forehead to break and drip with blood (Luke 22:44). The wildness of eye and the burden of soul that we saw as we joined him in the olive grove, it all makes sense now.

Hallelujah, for in the end, Jesus surrendered to his Father's will and resolutely faced this uncertain precipice. His Gethsemane's prayers, once a source of mystery and shame, now proclaim their own message: at his Father's bidding, the Son of God took on the divine burden of sin for those who put him there, including me—and you.

Jesus' prayer makes it clear: his death was definitely not an accident.

❤ A Prayer for the Heart

Jesus, thank you for letting go of your own will and for your resolve to carry sin's horrific burden. I worship and admire you for your courageous act of surrender. Yours is a prayer of one who has counted the cost and found your Father worthy of your surrender. The early church, knowing their lives were in constant danger, found refuge in your Gethsemane prayer, and so do persecuted believers facing death around the world today. I believe your will is always better than my best idea of what is right. Help my unbelief.

Reflect

How did this retelling help me to either better understand what happened on the cross, or affect my desire to pray like Jesus?

Lo Spagna, *Agony in the Garden*, 1500, Oil on Wood

A Word from Matthew (26:45-46)

Then he came to the disciples and said to them, "Are you still sleeping and taking your rest? See, the hour is at hand, and the Son of Man is betrayed into the hands of sinners. Get up. Let us be going. See, my betrayer is at hand."

James Speaks

For the third time that night, Jesus returned and found us all unable to ward off the sleepiness of the late-night hour. Yet our friend and intercessor awakened us with softer words than before. "Still sleeping and resting your weary bones?"

I blinked, then stood quickly, brushing dirt off my robe. My cheeks felt hot at having been found asleep yet again. I wasn't the only one among us embarrassed. John's eyes looked away. Peter prepared to justify himself.

Before any of us could open our mouths to apologize, Jesus continued speaking. "Friends, the time I have long predicted is here. The Son of Man is about to be betrayed into the hands of sinners."

Peter gasped and pointed. We all quickly turned around. We could see a torch through a gap in the trees, followed by many dark shadows. They were making their way across the Kidron valley, moving toward us like a snake preparing to strike her prey.

Our prayerful Lord knew they were coming and toward our garden hideout. He was never surprised. How easily Jesus could have chosen to wake us earlier and disappear into the night.

We walked back through the trees to where the other disciples had long slept without interruption. They were starting to stir. My hands shook as I began waking the last of our sleeping brothers. They, too, could now also hear the intruders approaching. They joined our careful whispering, trying to remain out of sight behind the trees. Jesus, on the other hand, was the picture of peace and confidence.

Standing tall out in the open, he looked at us and spoke at a volume that made clear he was not hiding or afraid: "Rise up, every one of you. It's time. My betrayer is now only a stone's throw away. I have been expecting his coming. Let the current of injustice rise. Enter with me onto the public stage whose events will soon be witnessed and remembered by the watching world."

Jesus clasped his hands behind his back as he approached the garden entrance. The sweat on his cheeks and forehead had dried. His gaze was steady as shadows and voices approached. He seemed to tower over us and this impending danger.

No question. The Master might be tired, but he was more than ready to embrace his Father's plan.

The contrast between his strengths and our weaknesses and frailty couldn't have been more evident. We were confused, frightened, and exhausted, all at the same time. Our hearts beat fast, and our eyes were still blurry with sleep. Since we'd failed to spend the night gaining strength and courage in prayer, all of us disciples were unprepared for the upcoming events of his arrest and march toward Calvary.

Yes, the crisis would soon crescendo, and when it did, we would decide to flee or fight. That night, none of us grasped how any of this could be the Father's unfolding plan for his Son and us!

Jesus' courageous resolution was the fruit of that night's long, heartfelt prayer. He was not in the least caught off guard by the betrayal of his dear friend Judas nor the schemes of the religious leaders.

Years later, we who had fallen asleep that evening would have our turn standing up for our Lord. Persecution and death marked our stories as we took his good news to the nations.

How soon we, too, would come to rely on the same kind of honest prayer and surrender that Jesus modeled this night. It was no accident that God used our suffering as part of his salvation plan for the world.

❤ A Prayer for the Heart

Jesus, when I imagine you that night, I hear a royal confidence in your tone. I see a heightened awareness in your gestures, and I bow my head in wonder. However, when I feel even a little afraid, misunderstood, or abandoned, I know that I respond differently from you.

Jesus, hear my confession. I want to learn to pray the way you prayed so I can stand firm as you did. Spirit, empower me. I believe you can teach me to pray in such a way that I will learn to face this life's giants as David faced his Goliath and as you faced down your fears. Help my unbelief.

Reflect

How might Jesus' courage to face his imminent suffering and betrayal help me when I face fear or a hard decision?

Duccio di Buoninsegna, *Betrayal of Jesus,* c. 1311, Tempera and Gold on Wood

A Word from Matthew (26:47)

While Jesus was still speaking, Judas, one of the twelve, arrived; and with him there was a large crowd with swords and clubs, from the chief priests, the scribes, and elders of the people.

Judas Speaks

hen the Passover meal ended, we worked together to clean the room and the dishes. Everyone was still preoccupied with trying to understand the meaning of our Master's new additions to our Passover rituals. Jesus stood up, cleared his throat and asked us all to go with him now to Gethsemane. I took a breath and felt my resolve quicken. My time to act had arrived.

Amid everyone preparing to leave, I slipped out to the street unnoticed. No one suspected I was headed to the Sanhedrin to betray the Master.

I took a deep breath of the cool night air, but my chest still felt heavy. Focused on arriving at my destination, I didn't stop to think about why. I also ignored the lump in my throat as I hurried through the quiet streets.

When I arrived at the high priest's dwelling, the doorkeeper recognized me and ushered me in. The elders sat together around the table, finishing their Passover meal. They were eager to hear my news; their eyes widened as I told them of Jesus' plan to go to Gethsemane. Yes, the Passover crowds could turn on them if they found out about Jesus' arrest, but the threat of Jesus to their well-controlled religious world now forced their hand. The risk had to be taken.

As for me, I was eager to see Jesus surprise them all. He wouldn't stay locked in a cage for long. He would once and for all rise up and show them his true power. Or so I thought. "This is ideal!" one of the elders exclaimed. He was right. The timing would be perfect with the last of the Passover revelers certainly in bed. And with Gethsemane outside the city walls, they could arrest Jesus with no risk of the sleeping crowds finding out. However, I knew just how devoted Jesus' disciples were to him. Peter, James, and John bore powerful muscles from years of hauling fish nets and fighting the outdoor elements. Several carried swords. And all of them were, in their own way, unpredictable and impulsive.

I warned the elders to take no chances and ensure their soldiers were ready for anything. The Sanhedrin's guards thus came armed with swords and clubs. If there were a scuffle with this band of untrained rebels, it would be suppressed quickly.

As the guards gathered and armed themselves, I tried to reassure myself repeatedly that Jesus' plan included revealing his strong hand. He would be glad I set the stage for his victorious revolution, right? I thought I knew better than he how things should unfold. In reality, I missed seeing the kind of revolutionary Jesus was.

Looking back, I see how masterfully Jesus' plan had been in motion the whole time. He knew the religious leaders would react with fear and suspicion to his ministry, no matter how peaceful his message and kingdom were. My greed and self-deceit had been more than apparent to him, but he never intervened. Far too late did all this become clear.

Please don't make the same mistake I did, friends. Reframe how you look at the Master and all the characters of this Calvary story. Can you now see that it was we, his betrayers, prosecutors, and executioners, who should have been tried, judged, and justly condemned?

Jesus, the Lamb of God and Son of Man, was the only one genuinely innocent. It would be easy to conclude that Jesus lost all control of his life when he was arrested but don't believe that for a minute. My betrayal and the Sanhedrin finding Jesus ready and waiting for them in the garden were not accidents to God. Together, they provided the next step in his plan to bring salvation to the broken world.

❤ A Prayer for the Heart

Lord, I live in a world where some people burn down church buildings; others even arrest and do violence against your followers. May those who are persecuted today be encouraged by how you stood up with only the sword of gentle confidence. May those who are beaten down one day be restored and their innocence be made known.

Lord, if the day should come when we face dangerous opposition or devastating persecution, I believe you will once again unveil your ultimate plan. Help my unbelief.

Reflect

How might this retelling make me more sympathetic, angry, or sad toward Judas?

Michelangelo da Caravaggio, *The Taking of Christ*, 1602, Oil on Canvas

A Word from Matthew (26:48-54)

Now his betrayer had given them a sign, saying, "Whomever I kiss, he is the one; seize him." Immediately he went up to Jesus and said, "Greetings, Rabbi!" and kissed him. But Jesus said to him, "Friend, why have you come?" Then they came and laid hands on Jesus and took him. And suddenly, one of those who were with Jesus stretched out his hand and drew his sword, struck the servant of the high priest, and cut off his ear. But Jesus said to him, "Put your sword in its place, for all who take the sword will perish by the sword. Or do you think that I cannot now pray to my Father, and he will provide me with more than twelve legions of angels? How then could the Scriptures be fulfilled, that it must happen thus?"

Malchus, the High Priest's Servant, Speaks

When Caiaphas assembled the group to arrest Jesus, he made it clear that everything must go exactly as planned. "What happens if you don't recognize Jesus in the dark? He must not slip away." Judas assured him, "He trusts me and calls me friend. The moonlight will provide enough light for me to recognize him. I will greet him with the kiss of friendship. The rest will be up to you."

As the hour approached, I stood by Caiaphas and watched as the soldiers armed themselves. Jesus was a blasphemer and mustn't be allowed to corrupt Yahweh's word any longer. Yes, justice was about to be done. My master turned to me. "You would like to go with them, wouldn't you? Then go, help arrest him, and bring me back a thorough eyewitness report." I thanked my master and promised perfect obedience to his wishes.

We began our short walk across the Kidron Valley, Judas leading the way. I did my best not to stumble over loose rocks and shrubs; the sound of a falling stone or a muffled cry might give us away. All our success rested on the element of surprise; one false move and our plot could be exposed to the city. If that happened, the uprising we feared since hearing the "Hosanna!" cries last Sunday could soon be upon us.

It was decided that Judas would go ahead of us while we remained hidden. We hardly dared to breathe when we arrived close to the garden's entrance and its olive trees. Judas entered the garden, and his torch revealed a man waiting for him. Though his figure was dim, he carried himself with dignity and quiet resolve. He was, of course, the one we sought.

Judas embraced him awkwardly, kissed him, and said, "Greetings, Rabbi." Jesus' gaze locked on Judas. There was no sign of surprise or anger. I breathed a sigh of relief as Jesus seemed unaware of our presence. His simple reply: "Friend, why have you come?" As Judas began his awkward reply, our leader decided the time to move had arrived. Judas' discomfort might give the whole plan away. We tried to enter the garden as quietly as possible, but the guards, dressed for battle and not for stealth, alerted them to our presence.

A muscular, weather-beaten man suddenly rushed out with a yell. Before I could move, he pulled out his sword and swung toward me. My head exploded in heat and pain. I lifted my hand to the spot and felt blood.

My ear was gone! My master was right. These men are traitors, hiding their violent plans behind talks of love and Jesus' claim to be the Messiah.

I felt dizzy. As my vision dimmed, the strangest thing happened. Through a haze of pain, I saw Jesus lay his hand on the brute's arm. Lowering his sword, Jesus bade all his followers to be still. He spoke as if he were in control, certainly not needing rescue.

"Put your sword away, Peter, and let me be taken. Remember, all who live by the sword will perish by the sword. I don't need to be rescued. This is no surprise to me. It is the plan of my Father. If I wanted to be saved from these men, I could pray to my Father, who would provide twelve legions of angels. I am in no danger, and neither are you."

Then the man I had come to arrest reached towards me and put his hand where my ear had been. Warmth flooded through me from his soft touch. The pain faded. My eyes began to swell with tears. As Jesus turned to face his arresters, I raised my hand to my head. Yahweh be praised, wonder of wonders, my ear was fully healed!

It was at Pentecost, several weeks later, that I would join the crowds who heard the one who had cut off my ear. His sermon invited me to an even greater healing—the mending of my heart. That day, Peter made me understand that Jesus' capture, betrayal, cross, and burial were no accident.

❤ A Prayer for the Heart

Jesus, I can empathize with Peter's use of his sword when he felt off guard and threatened. In the heat of an anxious moment, I can cut off people's words and feelings. Not you, though. When everything seemed out of control, you stood firm in gentleness. You called your betrayer "friend." You showed tenderness to one who would bring harm, even healing him. I believe your prayers will help me speak, stand, and live as you did. Help my unbelief.

Reflect

How might Jesus' example of embracing his arrest with nonviolence encourage those who face persecution today?

Anthony van Dyck, *Betrayal of Christ,* 1620, Oil on Canvas

A Word from Matthew (26:55-57)

In that hour Jesus said to the crowds, "Have you come out, as against a robber, with swords and clubs to take me? I sat daily with you, teaching in the temple, and you did not seize me. But all this was done that the Scriptures of the prophets might be fulfilled." Then all the disciples forsook him and fled. And those who had laid hold of Jesus led him away to Caiaphas the High Priest, where the scribes and the elders were assembled.

Malchus Speaks

My mind was still from the miracle that had just healed my severed ear; this was a moment and a man of compassion I would never forget. I lowered my hand from my ear and lifted my eyes to see him again not far from me. I could not help but stare and wonder if any others in my party had witnesses my miracle.

His voice could be easily heard in the night's stillness as our prisoner reassured his followers that he could have called down legions of rescuing angels if he wanted to avoid arrest. He then turned his attention to those of us who had accompanied Judas.

He held out his empty hands and reproved us gently. "Have you come out to arrest me as if I were a dangerous robber and criminal? Did you think you would need swords and clubs to subdue me and my followers?

"Day after day, I sat and taught in the temple unarmed, never rousing my audience to revolt or attack. If I were guilty or dangerous, you could have, and should have, arrested me then and there.

"Yes, this episode of violence was what you expected here tonight, but look at me now. Am I the leader resisting arrest or encouraging my followers to fight you? What evidence do you have tonight that I am dangerous? That you approached this garden under the cover of night validates everything I have been saying.

"Let me spell it out for you: your actions are part of my Father's plans. You are fulfilling the very scriptures you say you are so determined to protect."

The guards turned and glanced uncertainly toward the priests, who looked confused and more than a little sheepish. I felt foolish for participating in such a charade. Even ashamed.

The captain of the guard broke the spell and jolted us all out of our silence. He snapped his fingers and pointed us back to the garden's center stage. The soldiers grabbed Jesus, tied his hands tightly, and jerked the rope to lead him away. My heart sank as Jesus lunged forward and nearly fell from the sudden force.

Meanwhile, Jesus' disciples suddenly realized their danger. We hadn't planned to arrest them, but they didn't linger long enough to find that out. In the words of one of our prophets, they "scattered like sheep when their shepherd was taken away."

Their fleeing was no surprise to Jesus as this, too, happened just as he and our scriptures had predicted.

As I watched the soldiers roughly pulling Jesus down the path, I could see that though his hands were tied, he offered no resistance but rather an eagerness to comply with our wishes.

No matter his mission and motivation, I could see that the Nazarene's steps were his own. He walked on the path back to the city in a way that made it clear to everyone in our party: his arrest was no surprise or accident.

❤ A Prayer for the Heart

Lord Jesus, as your arresters walked you to the temple courts, I wonder how many of them grieved their actions. Did any of their misconceptions about you dissolve as they walked that path in silence? And how did Peter reflect on his own violence? Did the other ten weep after they abandoned you in this night's chaos? Of course I am part of this same story. I have resisted, if not run away, from the priorities and places you have called your followers.

Jesus, I again turn back toward you where I can confront my sin and grieve my lack of resolve. I believe that by grace, you can turn my ways of fleeing from you to a run straight toward you. Help my unbelief.

Reflect

What can I imagine Jesus thinking and feeling as he watched the disciples run away and leave him alone with his arresters?

Gerard van Honthorst, *Jesus Before the High Priest*, 1617, Oil on Canvas

A Word from Matthew (26:59-63)

Now the chief priests and the whole council were looking for false testimony against Jesus so that they might put him to death, but they found none, though many false witnesses came forward. At last two came forward and said, "This fellow said, 'I am able to destroy the temple of God and to build it in three days.'" The high priest stood up and said, "Have you no answer? What is it that they testify against you?" But Jesus was silent.

Nicodemus Speaks

I am Nicodemus, a member of the Sanhedrin, the governing council of the Jewish people. From the beginning of his public ministry, my religious colleagues felt threatened by Jesus. As for me, I will never forget the night I went to Jesus' dwelling. By the time we finished our conversation, his piercing wisdom had moved me deeply.

So when the council began to talk about arresting Jesus, accusing him of blasphemy and stirring trouble, I protested. We owed him a proper hearing as we would offer to anyone else. None of my brothers, however, would listen to me. When they moved to plotting his death, I'm ashamed to say that my fear of rejection won the day. I kept silent.

The Sanhedrin chose to arrest Jesus at night and then put him on trial immediately. Our law was clear; trials at night were illegal. How ironic! On the one hand, they were condemning Jesus for breaking the Sabbath law. On the other hand, they were utterly unconcerned about breaking the law themselves.

On the night Jesus was arrested, I sat waiting for the defendant with the rest of my colleagues. My heart beat fast, knowing his arrest would be secret and that the outcome of these proceedings would be death. But again, I was too intimidated to raise an objection at the time.

Suddenly, the doors opened, and guards shoved Jesus into our dimly lit room. His hands were bound, the hem of his robe dirty and torn. I clenched my fists. Why couldn't anyone else see how wrong this was?

And so our mock trial began. Earlier, aides had been sent to search high and low for anyone who would testify against Jesus, regardless of their trustworthiness. The council now pressed in, trying to produce evidence of Jesus' heretical teachings. Witness after witness came to testify against him, but their claims were outlandish and contradictory. My colleagues seemed restless, and I worried they might choose to go ahead with their guilty verdict even without proper evidence.

Eventually, two witnesses who could agree on something were found: Jesus had claimed he would destroy our beloved temple and restore it in three days.

I shook my head. Herod the Great, the master builder, had taken decades to build the temple at untold expense and labor. How could Jesus tear it down and rebuild it by himself—in just three days? "Preposterous!" my colleagues yelled. I had to agree. It would only be later that I would realize that, just like his phrase "born again," his prediction of a "destroyed temple" carried a deeper meaning. The temple he spoke of was, of course, not the building, but his body. Its tearing down and building up would be his imminent death and resurrection.

Nevertheless, even if we had understood Jesus' true meaning, the court would have considered his claim about the temple of God utterly preposterous and even heretical. All our treasured beliefs of God's presence were inseparable from this physical building.

Amid it all, Jesus did not bother responding to even one of our allegations. He knew the law as well as any of us and could have pointed out the illegitimacy of the whole proceeding or decimated the testimony of these witnesses. Instead, he spoke not a word. His strength and calmness made me feel that perhaps we were on trial and Jesus was the judge.

You who are under the impression that Jesus was rightly found guilty under Jewish law, think again. In the first place, no serious inquiry into the truth took place that night. The Sanhedrin simply sought to rid themselves of this Messianic imposter once for all.

Jesus intentionally submitted himself to our legal sham. The trial was just a necessary step in his Father's higher plan that, one day, many of us would be "born again." Our verdict and his death would be anything but an accident.

❦ A Prayer for the Heart

Precious Lord, the centuries of sacrifices in your temple found fulfillment in your final, spotless Passover sacrifice. Jesus, Lamb of God, you are now the rebuilt temple of God. In you, we dwell forever in communion with your Father. Thank you for being here on earth by your Spirit, in your body, the Church, and the ordinary places of our daily life. Jesus, I believe I can learn from my mistakes, see the deeper meaning of your truth, and stand up for you in a doubting crowd. Help my unbelief.

Reflect

What might Jesus have thought or felt while remaining silent before his accusers?

Giotto di Bondone, *The Mocking of Christ*, 1305, Fresco

A Word from Matthew (26:63b-66)

Then the high priest said to him, "I put you under oath before the living God, tell us if you are the Messiah, the Son of God." Jesus said to him, "You have said so. But I tell you, from now on you will see the Son of Man seated at the right hand of power and coming on the clouds of heaven." Then the high priest tore his clothes and said, "He has blasphemed! Why do we still need witnesses? You have now heard his blasphemy. What is your verdict?" They answered, "He deserves death."

Nicodemus Speaks

You might raise your eyebrows when I tell you that this long-standing member of the Sanhedrin is now an advocate for the accused Nazarene. Let me also be clear: I have never given up my commitment to every small detail of God's law. Allow me to share some examples of laws our leaders broke the night they determined to condemn Jesus.

I have already told you it was illegal for a criminal trial to be conducted at night. However, our scheme was more troublesome than that: our law allows no criminal trials during the entire week of holy Passover. You also need to know that no Jewish court could ask, much less compel, a criminal defendant to testify against himself. Evidence of guilt must be found and presented by others.

So, you will understand my shock when, not satisfied with his first three perversions of justice, Caiaphas demanded that Jesus give testimony against himself! But what testimony could he be asked to give? Caiaphas had nothing to go on; no violence or subversive plot of a political rebellion could be found on the Rabbi's record.

If, however, Jesus would claim to be the Son of God, no other evidence would be needed to put Jesus to death. Under Jewish law, such a claim would be blasphemy and demand capital punishment. So if Jesus was not the divine Messiah, his fate should be the same as a common murderer. Not content to simply make Jesus testify against himself, Caiaphas went further and demanded that he do so under oath. "Do you swear by God's name to tell the whole truth? Tell us before God if you are the Son of God."

We all gasped at hearing his question, knowing full well the life and death implications of his answer. As we waited, the room became quiet enough to hear the rustle of a robe or a slight scuff of a sandal.

I stared at Jesus, longing for him to say the sensible thing. He could so easily refuse to respond to this illegal question. However, what seemed reasonable to me, or to anyone else under the circumstances, pulled no weight for Jesus. He did not come to save his life, but to lay it down for others.

Though his whole future rested upon his answer, Jesus did not shrink in fear or stand up for his rights. Rather, he spoke with a penetrating majesty, "You are the one who says so. Yes, I declare that I am."

Caiaphas now had all he needed, but Jesus was not yet finished. Quoting from Daniel 7, our favorite reference to the coming Messiah, he continued, "I tell you, the day will arrive soon when you will see the Son of Man exalted with the Father seated at the right hand of power. I will one day come to earth on the clouds of heaven to bring my kingdom on earth."

In this end times image, Jesus added insult to injury by promising a future only the divine Messiah could accomplish. We were stunned at his courage and confidence.

Caiaphas' indignation boiled over as he rose to tear his garments, the traditional response of a high priest to a heretical claim of divinity. "Why do we need any witnesses? These blasphemous words are all we need to condemn him, don't you all agree?"

Easily swept away by Caiaphas' verdict, our assembly spoke in unison, "Yes! He is guilty and worthy of death." Even those of us who admired Jesus and sympathized with his teaching were too intimidated to protest. Caught up in the moment's passion, we all forgot about the law requiring a night to sleep on a guilty verdict—yet another neglect of our law.

Caiaphas would claim that our masquerade of justice would protect our people from harm; little did we know that Jesus' death sentence was no accident, but actually part of God's plan. We declared the Nazarene guilty of blasphemy, but it was we who were guilty—and it was for our guilt he chose to die.

A Prayer for the Heart

Jesus, I praise you for the dignity of your demeanor when you were unjustly accused. What strength you revealed in declaring your identity to a vicious jury! Yes, you are the Son of God. Let my lingering doubts find their shelter in the truth that you are who you say you are and in my every here and now. I believe that you can overlay my doubts with your courage so that I can confidently speak out your truth, no matter where I am or no matter the consequences. Help my unbelief.

Reflect

How might Jesus' courage to speak the truth inspire me in some way to do the same in my life right now?

James Tissot, *Christ is Mocked in the House of Caiaphas,* 1896, Watercolor and Graphite on Paper

A Word from Matthew (26:67-68)

Then they spat in his face and struck him; and some slapped him, saying, "Prophesy to us, you Messiah! Who is it that struck you?"

A Guard of the High Priest Speaks

y fellow guards and I stood in a line behind the accused man from Nazareth. It was a strange night, a strange trial. Something about it left me deeply troubled. I couldn't shake it.

My name is Ahaz, and I am a faithful servant of the high priest. I, too, had become furious when the prisoner made his blasphemous claims. My astonishment doubled, however, watching the fury of our usually dignified leaders. Their faces contorted with hatred; a number of them left their seats and crowded around Jesus.

Abandoning any pretense of respectability, several elders spat at him. As they shoved and hit him, I looked away. This man was defenseless. Yes, he was guilty, but their cruelty went beyond how a ruthless master might treat his disobedient dog.

What was going on here?

And they didn't just physically torment him. They mocked his supposed Messianic identity as he bowed his head in silence: "Hey, Prophet of God," they taunted, "tell us a prophecy you can fulfill right here among us. If you are the Messiah and Son of God, you will certainly have the power to know who it was that just hit you. Surely you know the things your eyes can't see!"

In response, silence, not rash words or self-defense, punctuated Jesus' response. Unsurprisingly, the council took his passivity as proof that he wasn't the Messiah. Certainly, angels would have come to rescue the true Holy One.

But I wondered...

Now, I am not pretending to be familiar with the nuances and fine points of Jewish law; people know I've certainly drunk more than my fair share of wine and told too many vulgar jokes. Still, as I watched the mockery and violence inflicted on this unresisting victim, I wondered, "How is this befitting of the high priests of Almighty God? Does Yahweh endorse this kind of abuse? Just who is innocent and guilty here of taking lightly the holiness of God?"

My respect and sympathy for Jesus grew as he submitted to our barbarous display with an air of royal dignity. As I watched, the words I had learned in my boyhood crept into my thoughts: "Many bulls surround me, strong bulls of Bashan encircle me. Roaring lions tearing their prey, open their mouths wide against me" (Psalm 22:12-13).

None of us saw it then, but much became apparent in the preaching of his disciple, Peter of Capernaum. In our irreverent bullying, Jesus was fulfilling the Psalms, the prophets, and his predictions that he would suffer here on earth. God's plan continued to move forward despite our elders' brutish behavior. It seems that none of the events of that night occurred by accident.

❤ A Prayer for the Heart

Jesus, the beating and bullying you received was what I deserved. What appeared to be weakness on your part was actually strength displayed for my rescue and well-being.

Lord, I praise you for your depth of character; clearly, nonviolence is not for the faint of heart like me. What a witness you were to the disciples and followers of the early church who were later subjected to the same treatment by the Roman authorities. What an inspiration you still are to persecuted Christ-followers today around the world.

Lord, empower us to love and forgive those who mock, exclude, or persecute your people. I believe you can teach me to love and live as you did, for this day and the days ahead I can't yet imagine. Help my unbelief.

Reflect

How can I personally relate to the guard being concerned about the experience of injustice done against someone innocent?

Carl Heinrich Bloch, *Peter's Denial*, 1865, Oil on Copper

A Word from Matthew (26:58, 69-75)

But Peter was following Jesus at a distance, as far as the courtyard of the high priest; and going inside, he sat with the guards in order to see how this would end. A servant girl came to him and said, "You also were with Jesus the Galilean." But he denied it before all of them, saying, "I do not know what you are talking about." When he went out to the porch, another servant girl saw him, and she said to the bystanders, "This man was with Jesus of Nazareth."

Again, he denied it with an oath, "I do not know the man." After a little while the bystanders came up and said to Peter, "Certainly you are also one of them, for your accent betrays you." Then he began to curse, and he swore an oath, "I do not know the man!" At that moment, the cock crowed. Then Peter remembered what Jesus had said: "Before the cock crows, you will deny me three times." And he went out and wept bitterly.

Peter Speaks

fraid for our lives, we all bolted from the garden like sheep being chased by wolves. I ran without looking over my shoulder until my aching side forced me to stop. Looking around, I realized that, in the panic and darkness, I had traveled in a direction away from my brothers.

In this place, I found myself safe but utterly alone. My earlier pledge of loyalty to Jesus came to mind: "Even if I must die, I will never leave you."

I covered my face with my hands, wanting to yell but still too afraid I might be found. There had to be something I could do to restore my honor and reverse my failure of courage.

I knew in my heart that I had to go back and follow Jesus to the bitter end, whatever the cost. I took a moment to breathe and look at the starry sky to orient myself before heading back toward Jerusalem.

I soon arrived at the high priest's house and heard several guards joking coarsely around the fire in the courtyard. Jesus was already inside. I saw no way into the house where I might witness the trial. I paused at the fire's edge to consider my next move.

As I settled in, I subtly congratulated myself for my newfound courage. If I were near the Master, I reasoned, perhaps another chance might surface to stand up for him. Yes, I still had my sword at my side.

It was impossible to stay hidden entirely in the moon's light and crackling fire. As I tried to get comfortable, a servant girl caught sight of me. Before I could turn to avoid her gaze, a knowing look came over her. "Here, now," she announced, "I've seen you before. You were with the Galilean preacher, weren't you?" Her voice carried in the courtyard's still air. All attention was fixed on me.

My mind went numb. I felt the same fear I experienced in the garden. If they found me, I could be found guilty by association and arrested on the spot. All my courage evaporated instantly.

The servant girl's suspicion grew as I fumbled for something to say that could deflect their attention: "I don't know what you are talking about."

Hoping to escape the stares, I moved across the courtyard toward the porch, trying to look as if I had somewhere to go. My attempt to go unnoticed failed. As the two guards turned their attention back to the fire, another servant girl moved closer and called out, "Surely, you know him! I saw you just the other day with the rabbi from Nazareth!"

I looked her in the eyes and tried to keep my voice steady. "You must be drunk! You are confusing me with someone else. I don't know this Jesus."

Trying not to look suspicious, I sat on a bench and took a slice of bread and some dates from my leather pouch. I was scared, not hungry, but my ruse worked. The servant and soldiers turned away from me and returned to their conversations.

Or so I thought.

Just when I thought they had forgotten me, some guards broke away from the fireside gossip. As they approached, one of them spoke up for the group. "We all agree; you were with Jesus of Nazareth. Your northern accent is a dead giveaway. You're from Galilee!"

Desperate and frightened, I blurted out, "I swear by heaven itself, and may I be cursed if I am lying...I have never even met this man, Jesus. Truly, I don't know what you are talking about!"

Where did these rash words of mine come from? My face flushed red with shame.

Only seconds later, the "cock crow"—the Roman garrison's trumpet signal—sounded, marking the end of the night and a change of the guard. As if Jesus were standing right beside me, I heard his prediction ring in my ears more clearly than the trumpet sound: "Before the cock crows, you will deny me three times."

Blinded by bitter tears, I stumbled away from the High Priest's house. My heart was already filled with shame and grief yet more overflowed. I had not considered myself or my faith capable of such frailty. Finding an empty courtyard near an abandoned dwelling, I slipped to the ground. I covered my face with clenched fists and wept like a child.

The light of truth would dawn later. If Jesus' predictions about my denials had come true, wouldn't his predictions about his death also transpire?

His repeated calm assertions that he would be handed over, abandoned, and then crucified were not dead-end parables. These prophetic words were coming true here and now at Caiaphas' house.

My failure should also send a clear message to any who see it as a reflection of Jesus' credibility. My weakness and denials were not accidental but fully predicted and woven into the Master's plan. He who turned water into wine would transform my bitter tears into a restoring oil poured over my leader's heart. I would arise on Pentecost a new man.

 ## A Prayer for the Heart

Lord Jesus, in our speech and deeds, in what we have done and not done, alone and in public, we have all denied you. Thank you for being in the business of transforming our failures into compassion and love. You welcome my shame, tears, and weaknesses and then translate them into assets. I don't know how your mercy works, but my deficits in your hands somehow make me a better servant.

Father God, your promise is that you already see me as glorious and whole because of Christ, your Son. So now make me to become who I already am in you. No matter my denials and struggles, Lord, you are molding me to make a difference in this world. If you did it with Peter, I believe you can do it with me. Help my unbelief.

Reflect

How have I made commitments, alone or as part of a group, and then failed to keep them?

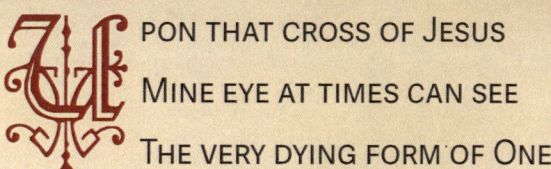PON THAT CROSS OF JESUS

MINE EYE AT TIMES CAN SEE

THE VERY DYING FORM OF ONE

WHO SUFFERED THERE FOR ME;

AND FROM MY STRICKEN HEART WITH TEARS

TWO WONDERS I CONFESS;

THE WONDERS OF REDEEMING LOVE

AND MY UNWORTHINESS.

- Elizabeth Clephane (1830-1869)

Rembrandt van Rijn, *Judas Returning the Silver*, 1629, Oil on Panel

A Word from Matthew (27:3-10)

When Judas, his betrayer, saw that Jesus was condemned, he repented and brought back the thirty pieces of silver to the chief priests and the elders. He said, "I have sinned by betraying innocent blood." But they said, "What is that to us? See to it yourself." Throwing down the pieces of silver in the temple, he departed; and he went and hanged himself. But the chief priests, taking the pieces of silver, said, "It is not lawful to put them into the treasury, since they are blood money." After conferring together, they used them to buy the potter's field as a place to bury foreigners. For this reason that field has been called the Field of Blood to this day. Then was fulfilled what had been spoken through the prophet Jeremiah, "And they took the thirty pieces of silver, the price of the one on whom a price had been set, on whom some of the people of Israel had set a price, and they gave them for the potter's field, as the Lord commanded me."

Judas Speaks

It was done. I had identified Jesus for the temple guards. My heart pounded as I followed the official group at a distance where the darkness could keep me hidden. A large knot formed in my stomach when we crossed over the Kidron Valley toward the house of the high priest.

When Jesus stumbled, they pulled him upright, yanking the rope that bound his hands. This rough treatment was hardly fitting. No, something about their manner was not right.

Having arrived at Caiaphas' dwelling, I followed them to the courtroom. Here, I would witness the brilliant defense I was convinced Jesus would give. I had long waited to see him display the Messiah's glory once and for all!

However, when I tried to enter the courtroom, a group of elders stopped me. "You have no official standing here. Only members of the Sanhedrin are allowed." I tried to protest, but they dismissed me like a lackey, overlooking how instrumental I had been to them.

I turned around, clenching my teeth and my fists in frustration. Hoping to avoid the guards who had mistreated Jesus, I wandered to the other side of Caiaphas' home. There, I found a smaller entrance where I could ask passing servants about the hearing's happenings inside.

Several minutes passed. I leaned in to listen, waiting for Jesus' display of brilliance and power to change the opinion of his opponents. I had hoped that Jesus would present himself in such a way the Jewish leaders would either burst into applause or sit stunned in silence.

Instead, harsh yelling and taunting words began to fill the distant air. I rushed to the doorway and overheard several people speaking as they walked out. "The Nazarene blasphemer deserves to be killed! If he can't even defend himself, that's proof enough of his guilt!"

I hurriedly made my way to the main entrance in time to see Jesus being led away, bloodied and silent. Something had gone very wrong. Things from there only got worse. I overheard the guards say that my former Master had been condemned to death and was now being taken to see Pontius Pilate.

This was Jesus, whose life I had shared for three years, who I followed all over the countryside. With my own ears, I had heard his winsome sermons. With my eyes, I had watched him heal the blind and calm an incredibly roaring sea. It was amazing.

And then the flashback: even as I betrayed Jesus, he had called me "friend." *Friend...*

The silver pieces the priests paid me now felt heavy in my pocket. I covered my face with my hands as a dark remorse washed over me. My gut curled in knots. Nausea set in. I took out a piece of the silver and stared at it in the moonlight. Were my eyes playing tricks on me? Its original shine seemed replaced by a repulsive blood-like film.

Disgusted and resolved, I tucked the coin away and buried my guilt out of sight.

I turned and walked directly into the room where the priests were still lingering and chatting about the trial. Drawing near a cluster of them, I stated frankly, "I have sinned by betraying Jesus into your hands! I can't keep your filthy money. Here, take it back."

"We will do no such thing with your blood money, Judas." they replied quickly. "What you do with it is your business now, not ours."

I should have known the priests would show me no compassion. Having taken from me what they wanted, they now saw me as a nuisance. Besides, according to our law, the bribe money could not be used for any religious purposes. As if anything could make them more unclean after the travesty they had just committed!

Filled with disgust, I slammed the coins down at the priest's feet and dashed into the street. I had hoped that ridding myself of the bloody silver would help relieve my guilt. Instead, the burden inside felt heavier than ever. The scarlet tinge I now imagined on the silver seemed to cling to my skin and even my clothes.

I convinced myself that relief would be impossible, that I could not live with the condemnation from my brothers that awaited me.

I walked toward the night bazaar, palms sweaty, hands shaking. In this unbearable agony, death seemed my only relief. Even the vendor who sold me the rope seemed to stare at me with loathing in his eyes. I was beginning to understand Jesus' earlier words to me, "Woe to the one who betrays the Son of Man."

I was long gone when the priests solved the problem posed by my blood money. They decided to buy a nearby field to be used as a burial place for unclean foreigners.

Did the priests realize they unknowingly fulfilled a Jeremiah prophecy when they bought that field? *"They took the thirty pieces of silver, the price of the one on whom a price had been set, on whom some of the people of Israel had set a price, and they gave them for the potter's field, as the Lord commanded me."*

Meanwhile, I left the marketplace intent on finding a deserted place for my next unholy purpose.

As I looked up and placed the noose around my neck, I could make out multiple crosses silhouetted against the sky on a nearby hill. Jesus would soon hang on one of them.

Clearly, the Master's plan for glory differed from my own. I could not at this moment imagine how Jesus had been in control of his destiny-even as I betrayed him. The blood money, the scheming, the potter's field, even my misery and despair were no accident. They, too, bear witness to the world of God's greater plan. My name may forever be a byword, but my testimony is true.

 ## A Prayer for the Heart

Lord, how I wish Judas could have known that a welcome awaited him in his Master's grace, that his worst transgression could never exceed your mercy. Yet I can, in some ways, relate to Judas. I become unsettled when things don't go according to my plan. Rather than feeling remorse for hurting your reputation, I often feel sorrow for the damage to my own. For that, too, I ask forgiveness.

Jesus, I come to you today. I believe each day you can open my heart to freely repent and receive forgiveness that I, like Judas, do not deserve. Help my unbelief.

Reflect

What might Judas' response to his betrayal reveal about the nature of unresolved guilt or shame?

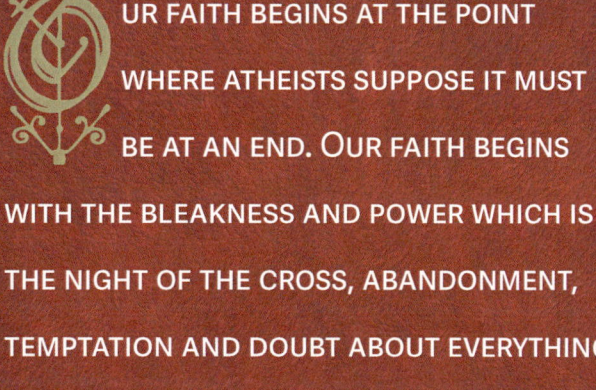

OUR FAITH BEGINS AT THE POINT WHERE ATHEISTS SUPPOSE IT MUST BE AT AN END. OUR FAITH BEGINS WITH THE BLEAKNESS AND POWER WHICH IS THE NIGHT OF THE CROSS, ABANDONMENT, TEMPTATION AND DOUBT ABOUT EVERYTHING THAT EXISTS! OUR FAITH MUST BE BORN WHERE IT IS ABANDONED BY ALL TANGIBLE REALITY. IT MUST BE BORN OF NOTHINGNESS.

- Elizabeth Clephane (1830-1869)

Tintoretto, *Jesus Before Pilate*, 1567, Oil on Canvas

A Word from Matthew (27:1-2, 11-14)

When morning came, all the chief priests and the elders of the people conferred together against Jesus in order to bring about his death. They bound him, led him away, and handed him over to Pilate the governor. Now Jesus stood before the governor; and the governor asked him, "Are you the King of the Jews?" Jesus said, "You say so." But when he was accused by the chief priests and elders, he did not answer. Then Pilate said to him, "Do you not hear how many accusations they make against you?" But he gave him no answer, not even to a single charge, so that the governor was greatly amazed.

Pilate, Governor of Palestine, Speaks

The Jews are difficult and complex subjects, always stubborn and arrogant, but I've found they are especially dangerous during Passover. I had long decided that indulging them, as my predecessors had done, was the wrong way to control them. After crucifying more than my fair share of the rebels, those who had complained saw who was in charge, and their initial resistance fizzled.

Still, I don't want Rome to think I have lost control here. I have since sought to find balance--keeping them under my power but still remaining on their good side.

I remember well the night when one of my men woke me and brought the prisoner Jesus to me from the previous night's trial. This defendant must have threatened their well-protected power; why else would they break their holy law by not waiting the whole twenty-four hours to finalize their verdict?

I dressed and thought more about this case; the real issue was probably another one of their religious disputes. But why would they want me to ensure his death sentence? I only have the authority to execute someone who has violated Roman law. If their case was indeed based on a religious dispute, I would gladly dismiss it.

The judgment hall doors flew open wide and I walked inside to take my usual place. Ironically, the meeting began with their religious zealots at the other entrance refusing to step into our Roman courtroom. They claimed it would make them ritually unclean before their God.

How irritating. I shook my head at their hypocrisy; they were illegally rushing this trial to a death sentence yet still insistent on keeping their Jewish laws so they could eat tomorrow's Passover dinner with a clear conscience!

The other Jewish leaders took their seats, which were arranged at what they must have deemed a sanitary distance across the room.

I looked at the defendant and compared his serene face to the frenzied accusations. None of their stated charges matched who appeared to me as a harmless, rural preacher.

When one of them yelled, "He claims to be King of the Jews," I sat up straight. I definitely could not dismiss this charge outright. Wanting to hear from him, I stood and inquired of the accused man, "So, are you the King of the Jews?" Jesus answered quietly as he met my gaze, "You have spoken the truth. I am the King of the Jews."

His countenance was clear and seemed to penetrate right into my soul. However, I detected no fanaticism, rebellion, hatred, or even the slightest bit of anger. My spies had no knowledge of any plot to overthrow Emperor Tiberius...so what did his words mean?

As the leaders continued their wild accusations, Jesus refused to say anything more. "Don't you hear what they are saying about you," I asked. "Why don't you defend yourself?" If he had spoken up, I would have easily granted him freedom, but alas, I couldn't get another word out of him. Searching his eyes, I started to suspect something more profound was happening here in the moment beyond my understanding. His resolve to die, even this travesty of justice, was, in his mind, no accident.

❤ A Prayer for the Heart

Thank you, Jesus, for the strength of your silence, prophesied by Isaiah so long ago: "He was silent and did not open his mouth, like a lamb that is led to the slaughter, like a sheep that is silent before his shearers" (Isaiah 53:8).

I spend much of my life defending my innocence, holding on to my rights, and protecting myself from injustice or being wrong. Jesus, forgive and have mercy on me. I admire your deep confidence that all was well when all the evidence seemed otherwise.

My King, amid life's chaos, teach me to pray and listen like you did. Lord, whenever I am tempted to be defensive, I believe you will help me to see and speak just like you did. Help my unbelief.

Reflect

How might Jesus' lack of rebuttal or defense speak to my experience of being misunderstood or misinterpreted by others?

Munkácsy Mihály, *Ecce Homo!*, 1896, Oil on Canvas

A Word from Matthew (27:15-18, 20-23)

Now at the festival, the governor was accustomed to release a prisoner for the crowd, anyone whom they wanted. At that time, they had a notorious prisoner, called Jesus Barabbas. So, after they had gathered, Pilate said to them, "Whom do you want me to release for you, Jesus Barabbas or Jesus who is called the Messiah?" For he realized it was out of jealousy that they had handed him over....Now the chief priests and the elders persuaded the crowds to ask for Barabbas and to have Jesus killed. The governor again said to them, "Which of the two do you want me to release for you?" And they said, "Barabbas." Pilate said to them, "Then what should I do with Jesus who is called Messiah?" All of them said, "Let him be crucified!" Then he asked, "Why, what evil has he done?" But they shouted all the more, "Let him be crucified!"

Barabbas, the Roman Traitor, Speaks

Before I was arrested, my mission as a zealot was to put an end to Roman rule in Israel and reinstate Jewish autonomy. I lost no sleep over cutting a throat or two. I viewed it as a necessary evil and a means to the greater end of Jewish freedom from oppression.

But one night, I was overconfident, and my carelessness led to my capture. For the month that I was imprisoned and waiting to be executed, the horror of my impending crucifixion kept me in dread day and night. It seemed no short time before the time of Passover, and my execution arrived.

Gossip among the prisoners brought unexpected good news. It had long been the custom on this holiday for the Roman governor of Palestine to set a prisoner free as part of the festivities. This served as a token of Roman mercy toward us Jews in their otherwise oppressive rule. And this year was special: the people would choose which prisoner to release.

Pilate would never set me free of his own volition, but if the people were free to decide, being a Jewish patriot raised my odds with my sympathetic brothers and sisters. I hoped they would pick me with all my being.

The night before I was scheduled to face my execution, the horror that still likely awaited me did more than keep me awake. Nightmares woke me up over and over and left me in a persistent cold sweat.

The following day, a guard opened the gate with a bang and yanked me off the ground. It was time. He tied my hands with a rope and practically dragged me out of my cell toward the plaza. I felt lightheaded. What if the people would choose to free someone else? Or what if they picked me, but that weasel Pilate didn't honor their choice?

I saw a disheveled-looking man on the platform as we entered the square. He stood bloodied and bruised, seemingly resigned to receive his death sentence. There was in him, though, a stillness and composure I had never witnessed—and believe me, I have seen plenty of men just before their deaths.

One of the guards barked out, "Which Jesus do you think will go free today, Brutus?"

Which Jesus? Wait. Was this prisoner Jesus of Nazareth, whom people in the streets had just days ago been hailing as our Messiah? Earlier this week, I joined many others in Jerusalem hoping this miracle man could awaken the Jewish people to action and throw off Roman rule. But looking at him across the way, this Jesus clearly didn't have a violent bone in his body.

So, why was he here if he wasn't a traitor caught plotting a coup?

I saw the Jewish priests and elders circulating in the crowd, whispering urgently to everyone they met and pointing up at Jesus and me. I was sure their hatred for law-breaking, murderous zealots was much stronger than any disagreement they might have experienced with this Messianic pretender. No matter how much air filled my lungs, I still felt powerless to breathe. The waiting was killing me.

Pilate first silenced and then addressed the crowd, "I have here two men named Jesus: the brigand and murderer Barabbas, and the one some call the Messiah, King of the Jews. To whom shall I show Roman mercy today?"

Though battered and bloody, Jesus' demeanor seemed to whisper: something else was happening here.

I realize now that my impression was more accurate than I realized. At that moment, however, I was focused most on the chances of my escape from death, which still seemed remote. From what I had heard about the Nazarene's teaching, mercy, miracles, and popularity with the masses, I was confident this crowd would call for his release. I didn't stand a chance next to him.

I tightened up as the crowd began shouting their reply to Pilate's question. And what was I now hearing? *Was it my name that was now echoing across the plaza?*

"Give us Barabbas!" they chanted.

I opened my eyes, not realizing that I had shut them. Pilate, as shocked as I was by their unexpected request, hushed the crowd and asked, "What would you then have me do with this innocent man called Jesus the Messiah?" Over and over, louder and louder, they shouted, "Crucify him!"

I was torn between incredible relief for my rescue and gnawing guilt from seeing the innocent Jesus beside me. I disagreed with his approach, sure, but he certainly did not deserve the cruel death of crucifixion!

I looked at him before leaving him to the fate that should have been mine. His eyes were now fixed on me. I expected to find shame, fear, betrayal, or anger there; I only saw mercy. In his eyes, I felt I was indeed Barabbas, a "son" of my Abba, my Father God.

Somehow, Jesus was neither guilty nor merely the victim of a capricious crowd, but rather part of a larger drama and script—larger than any of there knew. The exchange of his death for mine was clearly an act of divine compassion and, indeed, no accident.

❤ A Prayer for the Heart

Jesus, I accept the truth that I am like Barabbas, a traitor and rebel worthy of death. Like him, I am also, through your blood, now a precious child of your Father. Barabbas was set free because you died in his place and in my place.

Father God, though I do not deserve it, I am offered the Lamb's free gift of a second chance. I believe that I am forever kept safe in Christ from any fear, condemnation, or doubt about my precious standing with you. Help my unbelief.

Reflect

How might I in any way relate to the thoughts and feelings of Barabbas in this retelling?

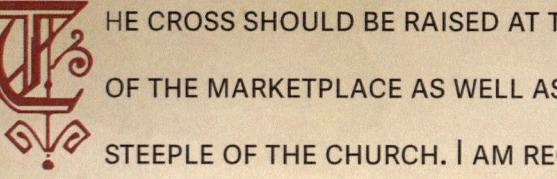THE CROSS SHOULD BE RAISED AT THE CENTER OF THE MARKETPLACE AS WELL AS ON THE STEEPLE OF THE CHURCH. I AM RECOVERING THE CLAIM THAT JESUS WAS NOT CRUCIFIED IN A CATHEDRAL BETWEEN TWO CANDLES, BUT ON A CROSS BETWEEN TWO THIEVES; ON THE TOWN'S GARBAGE HEAP; AT A CROSS-ROAD SO COSMOPOLITAN THEY HAD TO WRITE HIS TITLE IN HEBREW AND LATIN AND GREEK, AT THE KIND OF PLACE WHERE CYNICS TALK SMUT, AND THIEVES CURSE, AND SOLDIERS GAMBLE. BECAUSE THAT IS WHERE HE DIED, THAT IS WHAT HE DIED FOR, AND THAT IS WHAT HE DIED ABOUT. THAT IS WHERE CHURCH-PEOPLE OUGHT TO BE AND WHAT CHURCH-PEOPLE OUGHT TO BE ABOUT.

- George MacLeod (1895-1991)

James Tissot, *The Message of Pilate's Wife*, 1894, Watercolor and Graphite on Paper

A Word from Matthew (27:19)

While he was sitting on the judgment seat, his wife sent word to him, "Have nothing to do with that innocent man, for today I have suffered a great deal because of a dream about him."

Pilate's Wife Speaks

I am Claudia Procula, wife of Pontius Pilate. Though my husband does not generally discuss politics with me, I often hear him complain about what complex subjects the Jews are. His position in Palestine is precarious, and his hands are often tied. The trial of the Nazarene, however, stands out from all others. Its consequences are likely to still fall on our household.

On what I have come to think of as "that morning," I overslept. Pontius customarily arises at six o'clock, and I like to be up an hour earlier to ensure the household is in full motion and that the servants have prepared his breakfast. That night, however, my sleep had been troubled by a fearful dream, and when my eyes opened, the hour was later and the sky much brighter.

But sleeping in late wasn't what was on my mind. Instead, dread swept through my body.

I closed my eyes and tried to focus on my dream, but it quickly faded. One part, however, stayed in bold relief. I had a strong sense that my husband should be careful in his dealings with this Jesus, the so-called Messiah.

There was something in the dream about this man being innocent yet treated with cruelty. Having long heard that the gods speak to mortals in dreams, I was convinced I had been given a divine warning. If Pontius had anything to do with that injustice, it was clear that it would somehow be disastrous for us.

I dressed quickly and asked one of my servants to tell me where my husband was. "Pilate has already left for the judgment seat," he told me. "Early this morning, the Jews brought him a new criminal that they wanted to be executed as soon as possible."

Jesus! I was certain it was he! My heart was beating so hard I could feel the rush of blood in my ears and temples as I rushed to find Pontius.

When I arrived, I could see he was already positioned in what is known by all as the judgment seat. I paused in the entryway. It would be unseemly for me to interrupt; respectable Roman matrons do not get involved in politics, at least not in public. Besides, who would take seriously a warning from a woman's dream?

Still, I knew I must speak out. Gesturing to a nearby servant, I spoke an urgent message he was to deliver to my husband: "Leave that man from Nazareth alone! Dismiss the case if you must! He is innocent!"

My terror must have reached the servant because he walked quickly to the judgment seat and immediately whispered into Pilate's ear. My husband looked up and scanned the crowd, then turned toward me. For a brief moment, our eyes met from across the room. The expression on his face was conflicted; his eyebrows remained furrowed, but his eyes were gentle.

I hoped he might nod or give me some sign that he would heed my warning; instead, he turned to answer someone's question and did not look toward me again.

I saw a group of Roman women standing not far away and went to join them. I was in no mood for conversation, though. As I waited and watched from the shadows, I wondered what Roman god would have cared enough about this Galilean rebel to send such a dream to me. Might it have been the Jewish God Yahweh? If so, why would the dream come to me, a woman with no power, instead of my husband?

Out of the corner of my eye, I saw my husband stand and address the crowd. The people had a choice between either Jesus or Barabbas. I bit my lip and looked at my feet. Shouts swept across the crowd. "Barabbas! Barabbas!"

It ended up as I feared it would be. Jesus, an innocent man, was being rushed to a horrifying death, and I was helpless to stop it.

I looked at my husband. He looked confused, almost panicked—but he did not silence the crowd's cries. Dread and despair were within me. It was the same icy feeling from my dream. I shivered from head to toe.

Why would this man's God give me such a dream if I had no real power to stop the Sanhedrin's plot or Pontius' compromise? None of this made sense until the rumors of Jesus' resurrection days later. That was followed by a new movement emerging in Jerusalem. Slaves in my house told me of Peter's Pentecost sermon. After hearing the details, I knew my dream came from a divine source.

I had been right to feel uneasy about the death of this prisoner and the vulnerability of my husband to peer pressure. This much I know to be true: Jesus was innocent of the charges brought against him. It was an unjust death.

Could it be that this dream of mine helped reveal heaven's testimony that Jesus' death was no accident?

🪢 A Prayer for the Heart

Jesus, your Father's warning to Pilate's wife gives us a window into your innocence, affirming what we already knew. Father, your dream given to this unlikely woman reveals your plan and compassion. You were, of course, no mere distant spectator in these last hours of your Son's death. Spirit, come and speak to me too, even in the quiet turmoil of my own sleep. Lord, I believe your voice can warn, warm, enlighten, and surprise me, even in my dreams. Help my unbelief.

Reflect

Do I believe God can speak to me in dreams? What has been my experience?

And when I think,

that God, His Son not sparing,

sent Him to die, I scarce can take it in;

That on the Cross, my burden gladly bearing,

He bled and died, to take away my sin.

Then sings my soul, My Saviour God, to Thee,

"How great Thou art, How great Thou art."

Then sings my soul, My Saviour God, to Thee,

"How great Thou art, How great Thou art!"

– Carl Gustaf Boberg (1859-1940)

Duccio di Buoninsegna, *Pilate Washes His Hands*, 1311, Tempera on Wood

A Word from Matthew (27:24-26a)

So when Pilate saw that he could do nothing, but rather that a riot was beginning, he took some water and washed his hands before the crowd, saying, "I am innocent of this man's blood; see to it yourselves." Then the people as a whole answered, "His blood be on us and on our children!" So he released Barabbas for them.

A Visiting Galilean Speaks

y name is Daniel. Every year, my family and I journeyed from our small village to the city of Jerusalem for the Passover. Celebrating this holiday in the holy city was always the highlight of our year.

On this trip, chatter amongst travelers on the way had included questions surrounding Jesus of Nazareth. Rumor had it he was also on his way to Jerusalem. By no small amount of good luck, our village group arrived at the same time Jesus did! Lucky for us, or we would not have found a place to see him at the roadside edge. Crowds quickly swarmed, waving palm branches and crying out in praise. It was incredible!

While my family lingered at the market on Passover Friday, I followed the stream of people heading toward the judgment seat. Anticipation was brimming to know which prisoner Pilate would set free.

As we entered the larger square, there he was again—Jesus. Though, I couldn't believe what I was seeing. He was bound, bloodied, and silent. My heart sank. *How? What was happening? Could that really be the same Jesus?* I was sure God would never send us a weak, passive, and tattered Messiah.

Pilate rose and addressed the crowd, asking us who should be set free. The name "Barabbas!" began to echo around me. Every declaration of Jesus' innocence was matched by the crowd's "Crucify him!" chants. What a turning of the tables from just days before on the day we all laid down our palms and coats for him in the streets.

Further encouraged by the priests, their obvious impatience over Pilate's reluctance began to boil up. The mood was getting ugly. Even from a distance, I could tell the circumstances were causing the governor great distress. He appeared to be an animal caught in a trap, desperate for release.

Then Pilate did a strange thing. He brought out a basin filled with water and sat down. As the crowd watched, he moved his hand in and out of the water with exaggerated motions. All became very still and quiet. His voice stabbed into the silence, "See for yourselves that I declare myself clean before you and the gods. I wash myself from any consequences related to this innocent man being put to death. I take no responsibility for this case but rather pass off any of its guilt to you."

You would think his words would have awakened us all to what we were doing, but not so. Masses of Jewish Passover celebrants, including myself, were now all too eager to accept the mantle of responsibility. "His blood then be on us and our children! If our verdict is wrong, let us and those generations after us suffer the same sentence. But we are certainly not wrong! Jesus is not the Messiah!"

When the crowd began to disperse, I slowly returned to our inn, deep in thought as I walked, and quietly told my wife Rebekah what had happened. Her eyes filled with tears, for she had witnessed his loving compassion and healing firsthand.

By chance, several weeks after we returned home, I met some men who called themselves friends and disciples of Jesus. They told me about the corrupt priests, the mishandling of justice at Jesus' trial, and everything else that had followed Pilate's handwashing. They also told me of Jesus' resurrection with broad smiles and steady eyes.

I felt goosebumps from head to toe. Our cry that the blood of Jesus was to be upon us all brought to mind the Passover custom of spreading blood upon our doorposts. I joined my wife and boys in shedding tears for the execution of this innocent man whose death was somehow meant for us. I don't know how, but it's as if we were set free like Barabbas.

What my family and I could not see in Jerusalem has now become so clear: nothing that happened in Pilate's plaza was an accident, not even our shameful howling for the Nazarene's blood.

⊗ A Prayer for the Heart

Lord, your death comes as good news to me, my family and friends, and even those I do not know. You could have so easily washed your hands of us and said, "You deal with your own sin problem. It's not my responsibility." You were unswerving in fulfilling the Father's plan to remove the shame of our rebellion. I believe you can rescue me from the ditch of compromise and will help me walk faithfully daily and hand in hand with you on the road called integrity. Help my unbelief.

Reflect

How can I relate to Pilate's compromising on something he knew to be true or his need for the approval of others?

Michelangelo da Caravaggio, *Crowning with Thorns*, 1604, Oil on Canvas

A Word from Matthew (27:26-31)

After flogging Jesus, Pilate handed him over to be crucified. Then the soldiers of the governor took Jesus into the governor's headquarters, and they gathered the whole cohort around him. They stripped him and put a scarlet robe on him, and after twisting some thorns into a crown, they put it on his head. They put a reed in his right hand and knelt before him and mocked him, saying, "Hail, King of the Jews!" They spat on him, and took the reed and struck him on the head. After mocking him, they stripped him of the robe and put his own clothes on him.

Lucius Decimus Secundus, a Roman Soldier, Speaks

I have served Rome as a soldier for ten years, the last five in what we all call "the armpit of the Empire." What a disgusting place, this Palestine! Most of our subjected peoples learn to give in and put up with Roman rule. But not here! These cursed Jews! They whine, complain, and dare to call us unclean. Their religious festivals have become a convenient excuse to riot. They hungrily look for some military leader they call a Messiah to come and set them free from the world's most powerful empire.

Ha! I'd like to see them try to take their naive confidence in their local god and stage an uprising against Rome. Then they'd see what real oppression is!

By the time Governor Pilate finished pandering to the priests who brought in Jesus of Nazareth, my patrol and I were disgusted with these Jews. When Pilate told us to flog this prisoner who claimed to be their King, we couldn't believe our luck. We could now vent our anger toward a worthy target.

Brutus was our man for the task. His gruesome expertise was with the cat-o'-nine-tails, strips of leather embedded with broken bits of bone and glass. How well he knew his business! Scores of times, I've watched as he shredded chunks of flesh from victims' backs. Few can walk when it's over; I've seen many die on the spot. Today, though, we weren't to kill our man—just get him close.

We stripped Jesus to the waist, and Brutus gave him thirty-nine lashes, each one more savage in the hope of getting louder moans from the prisoner. Most victims beg for mercy, but not this one. His agony was obvious; it showed on his face and the blood ran from his back where hardly any skin remained. But there was no hate or defiance in his eyes. It was as if there was a space inside him where the violence of the lash could not reach.

When Brutus finished, he stared at Jesus and shook his head. Soon after, hands shaking, he dropped the whip. "Wait, I've got an idea." Quintus, another guard, left the room and returned a moment later with a rich red tunic. "Ecce! Behold! A garment fit for a king!"

Following his lead, we tore the clothes off Jesus' limp body and put the pretend robe on him. Some of us found a thorn bush and formed a crown from its twisted branches. We jammed the crown onto his head, pushing the thorns into his scalp until blood ran down his face. I found a long branch to use as a scepter and put it in his hand. We were now ready to give a mocking honor to this "mighty king." We knelt before him, crying, "Hail, King of the Jews!" I spat at him as if giving him a royal kiss or greeting. Others struck him on the face, feigning honor. In doing so, we all vented our pent-up anger toward these insolent Hebrews.

Still, no matter what, the Nazarene didn't resist. Though his face was blood-soaked, our eyes could still make contact. I was surprised—there was a gentleness in his expression. Though racked with pain, he still managed to see right into my soul and—*could it be?*—forgive me. Suddenly sickened at our barbaric display, I backed away.

I was relieved to hear Marius say, "All right, boys, the party's over. Get him ready." We saw in Jesus no anger or resentment, only a resigned patience. I watched the others tear the bloody robe and crown of thorns from Jesus' battered body and begin to dress him in his own clothes again. Though barely standing upright, he followed our every order without resistance, like a lamb for slaughter.

"Lucius, help us. Here, tie his robe," one of them motioned to me. A few moments ago, I would have synched the cord tightly around his waist, not caring that it would bite into the tender skin on his back. But now, I found myself gentler. We began to lead him out of the room. His steps, though faltering, seemed strangely purposeful, guided by an inner, ironclad will.

Something was happening that I didn't understand. I felt like a pawn in someone else's game. Perhaps none of this—the flogging, the mocking, the beating, Jesus' silence—was merely an accident?

❤ A Prayer for the Heart

Jesus, it hurts to say that in my heart lie the same seeds of anger that flourished in those who mocked you. Through this event, you invite me to worship you for your love of your enemies and pray for those who feel the sting of the world's disregard and verbal abuse. I believe you will help me love my enemies the way you did. Help my unbelief.

Reflect

What might the violence and irony of this scene lead me to more deeply appreciate about Jesus the King?

Tiziano Vecellio, *Christ Carrying the Cross*, 1565, Oil on Canvas

A Word from Matthew (27:31-32)

Then they led him away to crucify him. As they went out, they came upon a man from Cyrene named Simon; they compelled this man to carry his cross.

Simon of Cyrene, a Passover Visitor, Speaks

y name is Simon. My home is in Cyrene, the oldest and one of the most important cities in Rome's North African province. For years, it had been my dream to make the pilgrimage to our far-off Jerusalem, to walk the streets of King David and visit the tomb of our beloved matriarch, Rachel. Above all, it is the dream of every Jew living abroad to pray in the sacred space of Herod's temple, for it is there we can feel the special Holy Presence of our one true God.

For years, I saved and planned every last detail. Finally, I had enough for my dream: Passover in Jerusalem! Anticipation filled my heart as I prepared to celebrate our liberation from Egypt among so many of my people.

The first morning in the city, I woke early and purchased a dove for sacrifice. Naturally, I had come eager to experience God's presence as I walked into the enormous, majestic temple—how could it not? My heart, however, still felt empty. I prayed quickly and offered my purchased animal to the priests, still wondering what might be missing. Though I had never been to Jerusalem on Passover, the city seemed full of unusual excitement. I soon discovered that the talk of the town was about Jesus of Nazareth.

People present at his dramatic entry in Jerusalem had all heard the news of Jesus' recent countryside miracles. The rumors expanded to suggest he was the long-awaited Messiah, the heir of David, here to reestablish the kingdom of Israel.

It was joyful news for sure, but if it were true, I hoped he would wait to overthrow Rome's rule until I was safely home with family. I had come a long way for my unique Passover experience. Besides, I hate bloodshed.

The crowd's high-pitched expectations, however, were short-lived. I was running an errand when I heard that Jesus had been officially denounced as a fraud and sentenced by Pilate to crucifixion, a sign of both Rome's and Yahweh's condemnation.

After seeing a few people weeping and wailing in the streets, I decided to detour from my market plans and see what the commotion was about. I would keep my investigation short so there would be no chance of getting caught in any crossfire.

I could not have known what happened next. To make Jesus an example to other would-be Messiahs, the Romans decided to parade him on the longest possible road to exit the city. And here I found myself, right on the alley's edge, in the middle of their new route.

As I pushed myself forward, the crowd parted to make room for three men sweating under heavy cross beams. One of the criminals suddenly staggered and fell right in front of me, the heavy wood thudding as it hit the ground. Filled with pity and without thinking, I grasped his arm and helped him stand.

It didn't even occur to me that any association with his God-cursed fate would make me unclean and, therefore, unable to participate in Passover observances. Then the unthinkable happened. A Roman soldier pointed his spear toward me and commanded, "Get moving! Pick up this man's cross! You can carry it the rest of the way." My protests died in my throat as the soldier put his hand on the hilt of his sword.

What else could I do? Terrified, I heaved the roughly hewn beam of the cross onto my shoulder.

I began fighting back both fear and tears. Though unknown in this city, I didn't want anyone to associate me with these criminals. What would those watching me think? I've done nothing wrong!

"I'm innocent!" I wanted to shout.

The pathetic parade resumed. For a moment, I glanced back at the disheveled man whose heavy cross lay on my shoulders. Jesus' steps wavered, no doubt from the scourging. I looked closer at this blood-stained face. Free now from the wooden cross, he seemed to carry some other burden.

And then it happened. Jesus looked up and straight at me. Though red from sleeplessness, suffering, and sweat, his eyes communicated the most heartfelt love and tenderness I've ever known. I was overwhelmed by it! Here, in this unwanted situation, I finally experienced the presence of God--the prize that had so far eluded me in the supposed holy places of this city.

My burden lightened, though his remained. I hoped our silent fellowship and bearing his crossbeam on my shoulders might provide him a touch of comfort in his last hours.

After this fateful day and the mourning that followed, there were rumors that Jesus' dead body was missing, so I postponed my return trip home. I was invested now and I needed to know more. The town was abuzz with theories.

Weeks later, I would hear a sermon on Pentecost by Jesus' disciple Peter. He preached that Jesus was the final Passover Lamb who had come to carry the burden of the death we deserved. I was among the first who believed and received a new life.

This unlikely interruption on what is now called Good Friday became the turning point of my life. As his follower, I know I must decide to carry my own version of his cross every day. No doubt remains: neither my long walk with Jesus to Calvary nor his painful death there was an accident.

A Prayer for the Heart

Lord, I admit I prefer to stand in the crowd and watch your example or merely read about your sacrifice. Consciously or not, I want my life to unfold on easy street, without any significant loss of my happiness or comfort. I become quickly irritated when the needs of the weary and vulnerable inconvenience me.

Change my quest, Lord, to find the burdens of others I can share with you. Rearrange my heart and my routines. Empower me to join in the fellowship of your death by taking up your yoke and the appropriate burdens of others. I believe you will empower me to step out of my natural apathy and then help me every day to die to myself. Help my unbelief.

Reflect

What might it mean for Jesus' followers to join Simon by picking up and carrying his cross in our daily lives?

To some, the image of a pale body glimmering on a dark night whispers of defeat. What good is a God who does not control his Son's suffering? But another sound can be heard: the shout of a God crying out to human beings, "I LOVE YOU." Love was compressed for all history in that lonely figure on the cross, who said that he could call angels at any moment on a rescue mission, but chose not to.

— Philip Yancey

Matthias Grünewald, *Crucifixion*, 1516, Oil on Wood

A Word from Matthew (27:33-34)

They came to a place called Golgotha (which means Place of the Skull), and there they offered him wine to drink, mixed with gall; but when he tasted it, he would not drink it.

Lucius Decimus Secundus Speaks

arius, my commanding officer, ordered me to escort Jesus and two other criminals to the cross. I was still trying to understand the encounter I had at Jesus' flogging; even my hardened heart found it hard to look at his bloody, abused form as we prepared him for his execution.

But I'm a soldier and must do as I'm told.

Our place for crucifixion is located outside of the city's walls, next to the ever-burning trash heap. The local barbarian tongue calls it Golgotha, "the place of the skull." Not only is it splattered with the blood and bones of its victims, but the hill's rock formation is even said to resemble a skull. The stench of death mingles there with the scent of rotting garbage; it's disgusting but perhaps fitting for the worst type of execution imaginable that takes place here.

Calling crucifixion a slow, evil death by excruciating torture is no exaggeration.

First, we nail the victim's hands and feet to the beams with heavy spikes. The upright beam is then heaved up so its end can drop into a fitted hole. A short ledge below the victim's feet allows him the leverage needed to lift himself and breathe but at the cost of repeated agony in his hands and feet. The pain drives many of our victims insane well before they die.

Very few of the original crowds of curious onlookers can stomach the whole process. Rarely is there much of an audience for the last hours of the condemned.

As we walked, I drifted to the back of the procession. It seemed to take an eternity for these three condemned men to shuffle through the streets. I've heard the path has since come to be called the Via Dolorosa, the "Path of Sorrow." What an understatement.

Upon arrival at Golgotha's hilltop, as a token of Roman mercy, we offer prisoners a cheap brew of sour soldiers' wine made bitter by the myrrh. Knowing it will deaden at least a little of their impending pain, the prisoners receive it eagerly. So when our death parade reached its destination, I quickly prepared the cup of wine and myrrh and lifted it to Jesus' lips. Yet when he tasted what it was, he would not drink.

He even turned his face away. Exasperated, I asked, "Why won't you drink?" He did not answer, but once again, his eyes met mine. Compassion, not condemnation, emanated from his gaze. Why would he refuse this little comfort and subject himself to the entire pain of his crucifixion?

Might it be that Jesus' determination to drink the full cup of his agony pointed to a purpose not found in the thousands of other executions on this damned hill? Might this man's death be somehow more than an accident or the unpredictable justice of our gods?

 ## A Prayer for the Heart

Lord, I thank you for your unflinching courage to feel both your pain and ours fully. Your love leads you to join us fully in our suffering so that we might share in the fellowship of your sufferings. Jesus, this is a mystery and an invitation I am just beginning to understand.

May your loving presence awaken in me your courage to enter more fully into my own "Golgothas." I repent for numbing my life too often with busyness, platitudes, toys, and comfort. Inspired by your example, I believe I can honestly share in the cup of your suffering. Help my unbelief.

Reflect

What does Jesus' refusal to drink the deadening wine imply about his character?

Mongrammist H.C., *Gambling for Christ's Tunic, 17th Century*

A Word from Matthew (27:35-36)

When the soldiers had crucified him, they divided his clothes among themselves by casting lots; then they sat down there and kept watch over him.

Lucius Decimus Secundus Speaks

fter Jesus refused the wine, it was time. First, my comrades snatched away his garments. This was standard procedure for us; no point in wasting perfectly good clothing. As to the stains and splatters—what's a little blood to a soldier? Besides, gambling over a criminal's clothes gave us a way to pass the long hours of waiting for the wretches to finally give up and die.

We happily stripped our victims, first of their clothes and then of their dignity. This act was especially humiliating for the Jewish victims; they lacked our sensible Roman view of the earthly body as merely a shell for our immortal soul.

My fellow soldiers had just finished nailing Jesus' feet and hands to the beams of the cross. Usually, I would be there in the thick of it, maybe even driving the nails myself. Not this time. Today, I stood back, trying to distract myself from what I knew this Jesus prisoner was experiencing. A fellow soldier smirked, "Well, if those rebellious Jews thought this man was their king, no one is going to come and honor him now."

One of my comrades lifted Jesus' bloodied clothing, wryly asking us, "Who wants the cloak of a king?"

We walked a few paces away and began organizing the betting. Out of habit, I prayed to the gods for luck, but it occurred to me that if I did win this time, would I even wear the garment? Hardly. I would be haunted by those gentle but determined eyes and his iron determination to drink this cup of suffering to the dregs.

Let the others win tonight.

Thank the goddess Fortuna, when the lot finally fell on one of the other soldiers, the rest of us quickly returned to our post. In the interim, a larger-than-normal crowd had gathered to watch today's batch of victims.

A small band of the priests also showed up, looking smug and itching to shout their insults. We were surprised to see them, given how offensive dead and naked bodies are to their religion.

Some of the recently arrived women began wailing; a few men joined in with tears and moans of their own. Were they still hoping this poor dying man would save them? Ridiculous. It was time for them to let go and count their losses. They gambled and lost on this impostor.

A fair number of common country people trickled in from the city to join in watching Jesus suffer. Their faces carried anger and disappointment; they were the ones who worried me. Marius told the squad to look sharp, and I agreed with him. We are Roman soldiers with a reputation to uphold, even here in this scandalous place. There would be no surprises on our watch!

One of the religious leaders stood apart from his peers, closer to me, and eyes fixed on Jesus. I heard him mumble in shock, reciting something from memory: "They stare and gloat over me. They divide my clothes among themselves, and for my clothing, they cast lots."

Was this priest seeing a connection between our gambling for this imposter's clothes and their sacred Jewish texts?

I didn't know it then, but this day's events on the accursed Golgotha hill were making history.

I returned my attention to the next garment to be gambled for, but later, I could not help but think that this crucifixion had been anything but ordinary.

❤ A Prayer for the Heart

Christ, our Lord, and suffering servant, your enemies stripped you of your only possessions. They left you fully exposed to your skeptics' stares and jeers. Naked then but now robed in majesty, Jesus, Lamb of God, do not abandon those who are stripped of justice by their oppressors.

Jesus, you promise the day is coming when we will never abuse or oppress one another and never feel the shame of being deprived of our God-intended dignity. Despite what I see here and now, Lord, I believe the final day in your perfect time will come. Help my unbelief.

Reflect

Imagine what Mary, Jesus' mother, there at the foot of the cross, likely was feeling as she watched the soldiers gambling for the clothes of her naked son.

Diego Velasquez, *Christ on the Cross*, 1660, Oil on Canvas

A Word from Matthew (27:37-38)

Above his head, they placed the written charge against him. It read, "This is Jesus, the King of the Jews." Two rebels against Rome were crucified with him. One was on his right and one was on his left.

Barabbas Speaks

fter the crowd and Pilate set me free, I knew the smart thing to do: flee to the hills before they changed their minds! I pushed my way through the crowds who were smiling and giving me congratulatory pats on my shoulders. I just wanted out!

Though more than a little hungry, I had no money for provisions. Hide first, eat later, I thought. Yet when I reached the city walls, I looked at Calvary in the distance and stopped. I was the one, not Jesus of Nazareth, who should have been condemned to die on that hill today.

I stood there frozen for several minutes. *What could I do? What should I do?* At the very least, I realized that I owed my liberator a moment of acknowledgment before I headed out of the city. I turned and found the road towards Golgotha.

As I walked, I could see two crosses standing in the distance. The third was just being raised as I approached. On it was the Nazarene.

On arriving, I saw that the two crucified on either side of Jesus were fellow zealots and companions of mine. Their cries of agony were already piercing the late afternoon stillness.

One of the soldiers climbed up with wooden placards that declared the charge against each man to onlookers. Above my mates, the first two signs read, "Rebel Against Rome." The message was clear for all onlookers: Rome possessed no tolerance for resistance against its rule.

Retribution would be predictable, swift, and cruel. Jesus had not broken the customary laws rebels break, nor had he posed a threat to Rome's grip on the people. He was hardly a revolutionary. Still, the Sanhedrin are schemers and manipulators and seem to have a knack for getting the Romans to see things their way. I figured they had succeeded in leading Pilate to give Jesus the same verdict as these two criminals.

I was surprised when I read the sign they nailed to the top of his crossbeam: "This is Jesus, the King of the Jews." I clenched my teeth. Pilate was poking fun at my people's weakness and joking that this broken, naked, dying man before us was supposedly our king.

I looked around to see if others were as incensed as I was. Some in the crowd were likely those who, earlier that morning, had cried out, "Crucify him!" before Pilate. Their smug grins revealed their thoughts: Anyone claiming to be a king or messiah dies. It's the penalty for blasphemy.

It was stunning to see how the sign was affecting the religious leaders. Their faces had twisted into angry grimaces. Several started shouting at the guards. Then it became clear: Pilate had aimed the sign's barb at the religious leaders. I heard one of them demand the sign be changed to "Jesus, who claimed to be King of the Jews." The guard gave them Pilate's answer: "What's written is written." I nearly laughed out loud, delighting in this moment when our corrupt leaders did not get their way.

One more thing of note was that Jesus' placard was not written the same as the other two criminal signs in our everyday language of Aramaic; they were also inscribed in Latin and Greek. Why did Pilate go out of his way to proclaim Jesus as King of the Jews in the Empire's two most common languages?

I decided to change my plans and stay in Jerusalem. I had to learn more about this mysterious man who had taken my place so I could be set free. Pilate's unlikely placard had pointed the way for me and many others to wonder over and over again: *Was he our King? Could it be that this man who was crucified between two criminals did it with intention?*

❦ A Prayer for the Heart

Lamb of God, those who watched you suffer in weakness thought the curse of God lay upon you. Little could they ever know on their own that the creator and Lord of the universe hung before them.

Thank you for this sign hung above your head, this powerful proclamation from an unlikely source that you are King—King of the Jews, King of every tribe and ethnic group, King of all. May the message of this sign become truer and truer for me every day. I believe you will empower me to honor you as King in every decision. Help my unbelief.

Reflect

What might Barabbas' reflections on the sign nailed above Jesus help me better see or appreciate about Jesus' death?

Pieter Lastman, *The Crucifixion*, 1616, Oil on Panel

A Word from Matthew (27:39-44)

Those who passed by derided him, shaking their heads and saying, "You who would destroy the temple and build it in three days, save yourself! If you are the Son of God, come down from the cross." In the same way the chief priests also, along with the scribes and elders, were mocking him, saying, "He saved others; he cannot save himself. He is the King of Israel; let him come down from the cross now, and we will believe in him. He trusts in God; let God deliver him now, if he wants to; for he said, 'I am God's Son.'" The bandits who were crucified with him also taunted him in the same way.

John the Disciple Speaks

As I looked up toward my Master and dearest friend hanging on that cross, I forgot everything he had predicted about his death. Even if I had remembered, grief would have still overwhelmed me. Dying up above in agony was the one my soul loved most. With him went his beautiful dream for me and the whole world.

And if that weren't enough for one day, my mind kept returning to all the ways we had repeatedly failed him in his last and most lonely hours. Many bitter tears poured out of my eyes; they could not be stopped.

Slowly, sounds around me began to penetrate the fog of my misery. I looked around at all the spectators, enraged by the sign above Jesus declaring him "King of the Jews." Many in the crowd, I figured, must be visiting pilgrims who had come up the hill to look at the "Messianic impostor." They may have been shouting "Hosanna" last Sunday, but today, seeing Jesus on the cross, they were sneering: "You said you would destroy the Temple and rebuild it in three days. If you are the Son of God, you would come down from the cross, save yourself, rebuild the Temple, and then do whatever else you choose!"

"Yes, Jesus, if you did all that, we'd all believe you are the King of the Jews and Son of God!"

Anger welled up within me towards their ungrateful, ungrounded taunts. They would not speak thus if they knew my Jesus. In fact, their evil words sounded uncomfortably familiar. The Master had told us how Satan tempted him in the wilderness with that exact phrase, "If you are the son of God." The devil himself was the one who had encouraged Jesus to avoid suffering, be spectacular, and play into the narrow, selfish expectations of the crowd.

As I stood and looked back up at my broken, bleeding Lord, I wondered if their torments tempted him to come down and give them what their crass disrespect deserved. Maybe sending a legion of angels for a dramatic rescue would be a good start!

It has taken me many years to understand, but after that darkest of Fridays, the truth began to dawn in my mind and heart. Jesus could not give in to the devil's wilderness temptations to be a Messiah who would only be victorious and never suffer (Matthew 4:1-11).

If Jesus had saved himself from the cross, he could not have saved me or anyone else. Yes, Jesus' death is the only door through which the lost can find their way home.

And there's more.

By staying on the cross, by absorbing these thoughtless taunts, our sacred scriptures were fulfilled: "All who see me mock me, they hurl insults shaking their heads, saying, 'He trusts in the Lord, let the Lord rescue him, let him deliver him since he delights in him'…. O God, hear me…I am distraught at the enemy's voice and the wicked's stares. They revile me in their anger and bring down suffering upon me" (Psalms 22:7-8, 55:1, 3).

Our Master remained silent and nailed to the cross not out of weakness but as part of God's love and long-term, surprising plan. His choice to not come down from the cross was no accident. Instead, it was the fruit of a love I can never fathom.

A Prayer for the Heart

King Jesus, how did your love remain so firm in the face of such undeserved ridicule? The answer is found in the taunting words themselves, "He trusts in God." As in the wilderness with Satan, you trusted your Father and his Word.

Lord, thank you for refusing to come down from the cross, for not listening to the advice of the religious or the opinions of the crowd. How different the world would be today if you had not stood firm! Your example has since given courage to me, the apostles, and countless other sisters and brothers who have faced persecution and verbal abuse. With you as my source of courage, I believe I can stand firm no matter how people treat me. Help my unbelief.

Reflect

The devil was undoubtedly working the crowds and speaking his lies to those who taunted Jesus. What is a possible lie the enemy might be speaking to those who choose to ridicule Christ's followers today?

Matthew Grunewald, *Crucifixion*, 1525, Oil on Wood

A Word from Matthew (27:45-46)

From noon on, darkness came over the whole land until three in the afternoon. And about three o'clock Jesus cried with a loud voice, "Eli, Eli, lema sabachthani?" that is, "My God, My God, why have you forsaken me?"

Nicodemus Speaks

y God, my God, why have you forsaken me?" Terrible words they are, dark words, a prayer mingling the deepest despair, and an unquenchable flicker of faith. Jesus' Calvary bears witness that the Nazarene's death was like no other, for on the cross, he bore a burden that no other human would or could, I tell you.

Yes, Jesus' physical sufferings were gruesome for us who were there and watched. Yet, he was amongst thousands who had undergone crucifixion's horror and shame at the hands of our Roman occupiers. In the years to come, Peter himself would also be crucified, in fact, upside down. So please take a closer look at all of this with me, Israel's teacher.

On the day of Calvary, the sky darkened for three hours. The birds quieted. Everything felt eerie and still. How did this darkness come in the middle of the day? Why did it last so long? Passover occurs during a full moon, making a solar eclipse impossible. Frankly, all of us watching were too frightened by the darkness to even think logically about these questions. Even the ordinarily courageous Roman soldiers paced and shuffled with eyes toward the sky, wondering if the darkness was heaven's sign of Zeus' displeasure.

Weeks later, when I had settled down, I would remember the writings. They told of darkness during the first Passover, when Yahweh sent the plagues against Egypt. Three days of darkness covered the land, followed by the spirit of death, which took the firstborn son from every home not marked by the blood of the lamb.

I saw it, I tell you! Three hours of darkness that Friday afternoon preceded death, which took the Father's "firstborn" Son. Now, the blood of Jesus, the once-for-all Lamb of God, can spare us all from that same spirit of death. But there is more.

In the following months and years, the apostles and leaders of the early church agreed that these three hours of darkness revealed the uniqueness of Christ's sufferings. In those three interminable earthly hours, Jesus absorbed upon his perfect shoulders the accumulated consequences of humanity's past, present, and future iniquity. It was an inconceivable burden.

No wonder the darkness overtook Calvary's hill.

Then, finally, after hours of silence through the betrayal, the lies, the abuse, and the worst of the suffering, at the precise moment he had anticipated with such fear and resolve, Jesus spoke. He cried out with words that ripped the darkness and pierced every heart that heard them, *My God, my God, why have you forsaken me?*

Again, in these words of Jesus, we arrive at the threshold of mystery.

This was a cry like none other from the lips of Jesus in his earthly life. But given the burden of sin he endured and the bondage of sin he was breaking, no wonder he felt abandoned! No wonder these death moments ruptured his intimate experience of his Father's favor.

All people who feel lost and forsaken in their suffering can find in Jesus the God who knows their pain and never leaves them. Moreover, despite the darkness that lingers, Jesus can be trusted to hear our cries and bring us hope. Jesus' heartfelt cry declares divine evidence to the world: The purpose and experience of Jesus' suffering were like no other. Despite all that remains hidden, we know the darkness was no coincidence, and the cross was no accident.

And that is enough. More than enough.

❤ A Prayer for the Heart

Father, in Calvary's darkness, lay all the grief of every age's suffering—no wonder your Son felt forsaken. Thank you, Jesus, for your words, shouted in the darkness, "My God!" No, in the end, you were never entirely abandoned. The strength that helped you persevere under sin's burden is more than enough for us to carry our lighter burdens today.

I believe that in all my future trials, my testimony can be like Paul's: "I was persecuted but not forsaken, perplexed but not despairing, struck down but not destroyed" (2 Corinthians 4:16). Help, O Lord, my unbelief.

Reflect

How did this retelling help me better understand or appreciate the unique burden Jesus bore on the cross?

James Tissot, *The Death of Jesus*, 1894, Watercolor and Graphite on Paper

A Word from Matthew (27:47-50)

When some of the bystanders heard it, they said, "This man is calling for Elijah." At once one of them ran and got a sponge, filled it with sour wine, put it on a stick, and gave it to him to drink. But the others said, "Wait, let us see whether Elijah will come to save him." Then Jesus cried again with a loud voice and breathed his last.

Mary, Mother of Jesus, Speaks

 *y God! My God! What have they done to my son?*

I held him in my arms long ago as he smiled, cooed, and brimmed with new life. I covered his nakedness with swaddling clothes. Tonight, someone else will cover his lifeless naked body in a funeral shroud. I will hold him one last time in my arms, but his face will never smile again.

When my little Jesus was dedicated in the temple, old Simeon told me a sword would pierce my soul. If only a sword would pierce my heart instead so that I might die in place of him!

No such release, however, has come to me, only the piercing of my soul as bystanders mock my silent son. Mistaking his word Eloi ("my God") as Eli, they thought he was calling out for Elijah.

According to our prophet Malachi, Elijah would come back to life and announce the Messiah's return just before his arrival. And so the bystanders jeered, "We know Elijah will come to herald the Messiah when he comes. Let's wait and see if he rescues this pretender!"

Those who taunted Jesus missed something deeper! Elijah had symbolically come in my nephew John the Baptist, who had announced Jesus was the Messiah. I yearned to shout at them, to make them understand—but my voice was too hoarse from weeping.

Turning away from the mocking crowd, I looked up and saw my son gasping for his next breath. I ached to hear the sweetness of his beloved voice. I could not help but feel in my own body his ongoing pain: the loss of blood; the exposure to the sun, wind, and heat; the dislocated limbs from standing on nailed feet to breathe; the tearing of ligaments; the unimaginable burning of muscles.

On top of that, he had been given nothing to drink since yesterday's Passover dinner. His thirst was excruciating. Oh, how I longed to spare him from this!

My mother's heart felt gratitude when a bystander emerged from the crowd to lift a sponge of sour wine to his lips. Jesus sucked the sponge dry, not to soften the blow of his suffering but to gather strength so that every onlooker could hear well his final cry.

Those who heard it would possess even more evidence of what I already knew. My son was no blasphemer, nor did he deserve to die. When Jesus spoke his final words, a cry came from the deepest part of his heart, soul, and body. It rang out into the darkness and joined in with the earth that was about to shake: "It is finished."

My son, don't leave this world! There is so much unfinished, so much suffering that needs your salvation!

Later, we in the early church put more of the pieces together. His cry came at three o'clock that afternoon, the exact time the Passover lambs were being sacrificed in the temple.

Yes, realities would remain that need his healing: sin's residual shame and self-condemnation, our jealousy, our bondage to greed and cultural lies, and the old wineskin way of relating to God. All these would still define part of our human experience.

Nevertheless, in my son's cry, I could hear the tone of victory! If you listen closely, with the ears of faith, you will hear it, too. These final words, "It is finished," were not the last gasp of a defeated man.

I now know my son will always live in me, not just me; Jesus can live in the hearts and through the hands of all who believe. So, hear me proclaim it now, as my tears of sorrow have slowly turned to tears of hope: my son's embrace of suffering, shame, and death was no accident.

❤ A Prayer for the Heart

Lord, thank you for your unswerving love for us. You did not call on Elijah or angels or alcohol to relieve you from even one minute of your suffering. Calvary is holy ground, so I remove my shoes and worship you.

Jesus, I want the assurance that my bondage "is finished" and the freedom of truly seeing. With the words "it is finished" ringing in my heart, I want to grow into your likeness and steadfast character, even in the wind of adversity. Lord, I believe I can and will with you living in me! Help my unbelief.

Reflect

Ask God, "What burdens and struggles with my own history of sin are also finished?" Listen. Be thankful.

William Bell Scott, *The Rending of the Veil*, 1868, Watercolor on Paper

A Word from Matthew (27:51-53)

At that moment the curtain of the temple was torn in two, from top to bottom. The earth shook, and the rocks were split open. The tombs also were opened, and many bodies of the saints who had fallen asleep were raised. After his resurrection they came out of the tombs and entered the holy city and appeared to many.

Peter Speaks

hen Jesus breathed his last, it seemed the Father could no longer remain silent. The ground beneath Jerusalem began to shake as the reality of sin, now vanquished, spread over the earth. I was still hiding inside the city when the quake brought the city's buzz to a standstill. From my safe place, I peered out the window, hearing the screams of the onlookers returning for security inside Jerusalem's walls.

As the tremors increased, I fell to my hands and knees, no longer able to stand. Perhaps that was the point—getting back to our comfortable, "balanced" life was hardly the reason the Father sent his Son to die.

When the oil lamps in my room stopped swaying, I relaxed and reflected. This quake on earth was a sign from heaven to point us to the truth. God was harnessing his world to give voice to the meaning of his Son's death. Our thick city walls couldn't keep out the Father's declaration of the new era his Son was inaugurating!

During my Master's ministry, ample signs from heaven offered evidence that he was indeed the Son of God. We saw a withered hand restored, a dead man awakened, a dangerous storm calmed, and a paralytic walking, to name just a few. Add this earthquake now! Still, the Father was not finished. Two more signs soon came that also proclaimed the divine purpose behind Jesus' death.

At the same time as the earth's shaking, the six-inch thick, floor-to-ceiling temple curtain was ripped from top to bottom as if it were a mere garment.

For those unfamiliar with our Jewish Temple, this curtain separated the rest of the Temple from the inner sanctum called "the Holy of Holies." No human could enter the sacred space, not even the high priest, except on the annual Day of Atonement ceremony. The curtain had long symbolized God's holiness. It reminded our people that a real connection to God was possible, but close contact was not.

The message of this miracle was clear to us Jews, and the implications jolted our long-held assumption that Jesus' unique sacrifice now made God's mercy and presence intimately available. A wall was no longer needed! This was amazing!

As one of my brothers later wrote, we could now "draw near with confidence to the throne of grace that we might receive mercy and find grace to help in time of need" (Hebrews 4:16). Well said, but our religious leaders would disagree; our limited access to God provided them job security.

Still, our God wasn't finished. There was a third miracle, a third sign, perhaps the most awesome of all! *How do I put this into words?*

The severe tremors had cracked many tombstones. Bodies of saints long buried came forth from under the broken gravestones. Alive and restored, they walked the streets of Jerusalem! The truth, I tell you!

Skeptics, hear this: Many witnesses saw these living saints. The impact of our Master's victory went backward and forward in time, splitting it along with the stones and the tombs! This sign declared once and for all that death was conquered by the Author of Life. The picture of this fateful Friday was now complete.

Three previous signposts had signaled Christ's death before it happened: the Lord's Supper, the Gethsemane prayer, and Jesus' cry of forsakenness. Though hidden from public view, these revealed to us disciples Calvary's divine purpose. And now, just after Christ's death, these public miracles provided three more signposts. Together, they all form undeniable evidence that what happened to my Master on Golgotha was no accident!

A Prayer for the Heart

Lord Jesus, when you breathed your last, the earth could remain silent no longer. In solidarity with her maker, she cried out. Those who rose from their graves bore visible and verbal witness of your victory over death. You plan to make your ongoing victory visible and verbal by sending people like me into a watching world. Amid life's ongoing earthquakes of change and grief, may you make us into signs that will persuade even the skeptics.

Lord, I believe that I, too, with all my imperfections, can be a visible witness that you are the hope of the world. Jesus, help my unbelief.

Reflect

What might I have felt or thought if I had been a Passover visitor to Jerusalem and experienced these three signs?

James Tissot, *Confession of the Centurion*, 1894, Watercolor and Graphite on Paper

A Word from Matthew (27:54)

Now when the centurion and those with him, who were keeping watch over Jesus, saw the earthquake and what took place, they were terrified and said, "Truly this man was God's Son!"

Gaius Marcellus, a Roman Centurion, Speaks

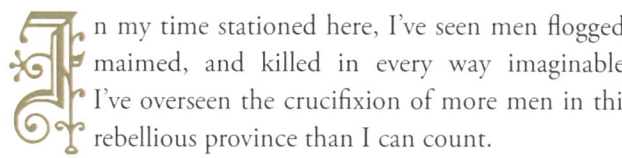

In my time stationed here, I've seen men flogged, maimed, and killed in every way imaginable. I've overseen the crucifixion of more men in this rebellious province than I can count.

I say this not as a badge of honor but to establish my credentials. I know how men die.

But this crucifixion, this death, was different from beginning to end. I watched Jesus refuse to beg for mercy as he was flogged and mocked by my troops. I saw his determined steps as he staggered to Golgotha and heard the prayer he offered to his God to forgive his enemies—to forgive me, the leader of his tormentors!

I marveled at his refusal of our offering of cheap wine to deaden some of his pain. I heard his strange and comforting words about paradise to a criminal he didn't know. Even as he writhed in pain, he expressed tender concern toward his mother. I heard his heartfelt cry of desolation directed heavenward and his final shout, "It is finished!"

When the sky darkened black, my heart began to race. This was no ordinary solar eclipse.

I ordered some soldiers to light torches against the strange midday twilight. In the shadow, I looked at the troops under my command. Some of them shifted from foot to foot; their anxiety made it impossible to stand still. I saw one of my fellow officers sweating; another repeatedly swallowed hard and cleared his throat as both eyes gazed downward.

Many kept looking at the place in the sky where the sun should have been shining, where the gods were supposed to reign. Not a sound, however, did they offer.

An hour or so later, when Jesus' head slumped forward with his last breath, the ground began to shake. Rocks clattered down the hillside, and shouts of fear pierced the air. In the midst of the chaos, I stopped and looked up at this Jesus of Nazareth. Out of my mouth, almost involuntarily, came my verdict: "Truly, this man was God's Son!"

Why did the Sanhedrin, the people's religious leaders, miss the obvious? Was it not their job to guide people to truth and to God? And what about his close followers? One was here with Jesus' mother this afternoon, but he seemed as downcast and confused as anyone.

What blinded those in Jesus' inner circle to the truth about Jesus' identity? It's not clear to me. So then, why did I, an unlikely and unclean Gentile, one of their enemies, end up being the first witness to declare the truth about Jesus?

As I said before, I had put so many men to death that I could easily see the difference in how this one died. My second qualification, perhaps, was this: I had no fear of repercussions or personal agenda to prevent me from speaking this truth in public.

Jesus was killed because he claimed to be the Son of God. I, Gaius Marcellus, the Roman Centurion, recognized that Jesus was, in fact, who he said he was. By the way, many other Gentiles like me would come to the same conclusion in the months and years ahead.

I leave you who are seeking justice with this final thought: If Jesus' death revealed he was the Son of God, then who is truly guilty and who is innocent? Jesus revealed something divine and stunning in his death, even to us Gentiles. So then, how could the death of this Jewish victim be a mere accident?

A Prayer for the Heart

Jesus, forgive me when I, too, am slow to recognize or speak the plain truth of your identity. Jesus, I haven't seen any earthquakes or people risen from the dead, but I have seen your work in my life and the lives of my sisters and brothers. I know enough to be a witness to this world that so profoundly misunderstands who you indeed are. Deep inside, I believe you can use me, like the Roman centurion, to declare your testimony in courageous words and deeds. Help my unbelief.

Reflect

Try to imagine the Roman centurion having a conversation with Mary and John soon after Jesus died. What might he have said or asked of them?

Tintoretto, *Lamentation over the Dead Christ*, 1560,
Oil on Canvas

A Word from Matthew (27:55-61)

Many women were also there, looking on from a distance; they had followed Jesus from Galilee and had provided for him. Among them were Mary Magdalene, Mary the mother of James and Joseph, and the mother of the sons of Zebedee. When it was evening, there came a rich man from Arimathea, named Joseph, who was also a disciple of Jesus. He went to Pilate and asked for the body of Jesus; then Pilate ordered it to be given to him. So Joseph took the body and wrapped it in a clean linen cloth and laid it in his own new tomb, which he had hewn in the rock. He then rolled a great stone to the door of the tomb and went away. Mary Magdalene and the other Mary were there, sitting opposite the tomb.

Joseph of Arimathea, Member of the Sanhedrin, Speaks

I come from a wealthy family that has lived and died in Arimathea, a village just north of Jerusalem, for generations. I secured a coveted seat on the Sanhedrin through family connections, though I was never cut from the same religious cloth as my colleagues.

When I first heard Jesus preach, his words created a thirst in me beyond the Sanhedrin's narrow focus on purity laws and public piety. A year later, knowing more about Jesus and what it would cost to follow him, I secretly became his disciple.

I watched our Master's death from a safe distance. It was dangerous to be seen as an ally of the supposed blasphemer. However, the women, transformed by his love and touch, never left. They stayed there at the cross to the very end.

After Jesus breathed his last and the earth stopped shaking, I prepared to head back toward the city gate. No one wants to stay around and see the Romans break the legs of those not yet dead and then wrench the corpses off their crosses. I leaned down to adjust the straps on my sandals for the walk.

But as I stood back up, I saw three women looking up silently at Jesus' body. I recognized one of them as Jesus' mother as she slowly rose from her kneeling position. As she wiped her eyes, another woman put an arm around her shoulders. Instead of heading back into Jerusalem, I turned and walked back up to join them.

"Please. Is there anything I can do to help?"

The younger woman with bloodshot eyes and pale streaks on her dusty cheeks cleared her throat. "Yes, there is a way you could help us."

They wanted to perform one last service for Jesus by bathing and anointing his body for burial. According to our law, we cannot leave a dead body outside overnight, nor can we do work on the Sabbath. To be able to come back and do their duty, the women needed to know where Jesus' body would be taken. But neither they nor I had any idea what the Romans or the Jews would do with Jesus' corpse. The rabbi from Galilee now seemed abandoned. Something in me stirred...

"I can do more than find out where he will be buried," I offered. "I can provide a place where his body can rest with honor. I will send word once all is settled."

The women clutched their hearts and nodded in evident gratitude.

With sundown approaching fast, I could not waste a minute. I hurried toward the city, making straight for Pontius Pilate's dwelling. Thanks to my position on the Sanhedrin, I was ushered in right away to see him. I knew that I might be seen guilty by associating with the one just crucified, but I stood firm and asked permission to bury Jesus' body in my own tomb.

"Yes, yes, of course," Pilate said, nodding. He was only too happy to grant my request and finally be done with the whole troublesome situation. I thanked him and returned home to ask my servants for help.

After returning to the hill of his execution, we carefully wrapped his body before taking it to my tomb and laying it carefully inside. We then rolled the heavy stone in its groove down the incline and over the entrance.

His burial was finished.

It was only later I realized that in this simple action, I was fulfilling one of Isaiah's overlooked prophecies: *"He was with a rich man in his death"* (Isaiah 53:9). Add this as one more reason I will follow him, one more piece of evidence that Jesus' death, even his burial, was no accident.

❤ A Prayer for the Heart

Jesus, I acknowledge that being human means we will all die and our human bodies be discarded. Honestly, I would rather not think about it because it's a harsh reality. In your burial, I am invited to have courage to face my end. Joseph's example inspires people of all ages to give and live without worrying about how others will think or react.

In you, Christ, I do not need to fear my own death and mortality. And if that's true, I believe I can live generously and give freely today without fear of the consequences. Help my unbelief.

Reflect

What might be one thing I could make available to others without fear of what people say or think?

Tissot, *The Watch Over the Tomb*, 1886, Opaque Watercolor over Graphite on Paper

A Word from Matthew (27:62-66)

The next day, that is, after the Day of Preparation, the chief priests and the Pharisees gathered before Pilate and said, "Sir, we remember what that impostor said while he was still alive, 'After three days I will rise again.' Therefore command the tomb to be made secure until the third day; otherwise his disciples may go and steal him away, and tell the people, 'He has been raised from the dead,' and the last deception would be worse than the first." Pilate said to them, "You have a guard of soldiers; go, make it as secure as you can." So they went with the guard and made the tomb secure by sealing the stone.

Joseph of Arimathea Speaks

After the heavy stone for the tomb rolled into its groove, gratitude welled in my heart for the chance to have been helpful to my Lord. Discouragement and despair soon crept in, though. With Jesus dead, my greatest hope in life felt crushed and shattered.

Neither the women nor I wanted to say it aloud, but we all realized it was time to move on, end this chapter, and count our losses.

A few hours later, as I was sitting alone with my grief, I heard a knock at my door. *Who could that be?* I opened the door to find a small band of temple guards showing me orders written by Caiaphas' own hand. They had sent with Pilate's permission to guard the tomb of Jesus for the next three days. The guards were also commanded to answer no questions.

What could our high pirest and Sanhedrin leaders be so worried about, even after his death? I was more than curious—I was disturbed.

After a restless night's sleep, I went early to the temple area. A lone temple guard told me that the leaders of the Sanhedrin had visited Pilate just hours after I did on Friday. He was quick to add the obvious that in doing so, they had broke their own strict purity law and made themselves unclean for the Sabbath.

The threat of Jesus' popularity led them once again to compromise their convictions about keeping God's laws, even after he was dead.

The guard went on to tell me the Sanhedrin leaders asked that Roman soldiers be posted—an unusual request. Here is the heart of what he heard them say:

"We don't believe that Jesus will rise in three days as he predicted, but if his disciples were to come and steal his body, they could deceive the gullible crowds into believing he had risen. That deception might be enough to incite the crowds to a greater disruption than last week. Pilate does not want that to happen, and neither do we."

It was hard to hear. Even with Jesus gone, the religious leaders never relented from their plotting and determination to regain control over the people. *I am disgusted to even be associated with them.*

The temple guard continued with his story. Apparently, the religious leaders knew how to get what they wanted from Pilate. Their wish was quickly granted. With permission granted by Roman authority, they were free to put the last installment of their scheming plans into motion. One of their spies reported where Jesus' body had been taken, and a small band of Pilate's soldiers were dispatched to my burial tomb.

No one would be allowed near it, day or night.

So now I knew their motive, but I was helpless to speed up the guard's departure from my property.

The next day, Sunday, the women returned early and found the guards there. And, of course, they found much more! No one had entered the area, but somehow the stone had been quietly rolled away. Our Master had risen from the dead!

It became clear to us that if the guards had not been posted, our religious leaders could have challenged the integrity of the news that Jesus is risen. How ironic! What Caiaphas chose as the means to finally close the story of Jesus, God wove into his plan to bear witness to the truth that all was made new.

Yes, his Son is risen indeed! The posting of the guard was no accident but a final twist in God's ongoing counterplot of his Son's world-altering death.

🧡 A Prayer for the Heart

Lord of history, this story of the guarded tomb encourages me. It's easy to look out in the world and be aware of so many human endeavors that are done without thought of you. It's easy to wonder how your plan can fight through our scheming and win out. Thank you for this story, for the reminder once again that "all things work together for good for those who love" and follow you. I believe you can keep me attentive and hopeful no matter how bad the news is or how little your name is honored or remembered. Help my unbelief.

Reflect

What did this retelling of the posted guards help me better appreciate about the story and truth of Jesus' death?

Benjamin West, *The Women at the Sepulchre*, 1805, Oil on Panel

A Word from Matthew (28:1-6)

After the Sabbath, as the first day of the week was dawning, Mary Magdalene and the other Mary went to see the tomb. And suddenly there was a great earthquake; for an angel of the Lord, descending from heaven, came and rolled back the stone and sat on it. His appearance was like lightning and his clothing white as snow. For fear of him the guards shook and became like dead men. But the angel said to the women, "Do not be afraid; I know that you are looking for Jesus who was crucified. He is not here; for he has been raised, as he said. Come, see the place where he lay."

Mary Magdalene Speaks

From the moment Jesus drove out my seven demons, I have loved and followed him. His arrest and death came so unexpectedly; the body of my beloved Master came off the cross crushed and lifeless.

I remember staring up at his limp, broken body with his mother, Mary, trembling next to me. I wept, sure that all my hopes had been burned to ashes. On the Sabbath day after Jesus' death, we could do nothing but grieve—and deeply grieve we did, especially his mother.

When the sun appeared the following day, its rays could not diminish our despair. We were certain true light would never dawn again. Everything was dim. My soul echoed with his final cry, "My God, why have you forsaken me?" Jesus' predictions of rising from the dead had faded from my memory and could offer me no comfort.

My determination to honor my Lord, however, did not waver. Sunday, at dawn, several women joined me in collecting linen and spices to take to the tomb. The thought of seeing his bloody, lifeless body was pushed aside by our unwavering commitment to this last act of loving service.

When we arrived, those Roman soldiers guarding the premises could see we were no threat and let us pass. They asked us how we would remove the stone without their help. Our walking slowed as we pondered the question. *If they didn't move it, how would we get inside the tomb?* We hadn't thought about how we would push aside the stone ourselves.

We immediately got the answer! A violent earthquake shook the ground under our feet. I cried out, grasped Mary's arm, and then looked up to see, glory to God, a being that stood beside the tomb. He could only be an angel dressed in a white garment more radiant than the purest snow! The early rays of sunlight reflected off him, illuminating the ground beneath his feet. My mouth hung open as he effortlessly rolled away the stone from its groove at the tomb's entrance.

As the tomb was opened, the Roman guards turned, intending to run far away, but ended up falling face down, unable to move or look up. Our group of women were equally afraid, but our feet would not move. The white of our faces must have matched the white of the angel's garments.

The angel spoke to us, eye to eye, "Do not be afraid! I am from God. All of heaven knows why you came this morning; you are looking for the dead body of Jesus. Your mission this morning is no longer to anoint his body but to come in and see for yourselves that he has risen. You are surprised, but you should not be. Jesus told you all that after he suffered and died, he would rise from the dead."

And so, in that garden, on the first day of the week, the light of a new creation dawned right before us.

We edged forward, aching to believe. Our vision slowly adjusted to the darkness as we crouched down to enter the tomb. We saw with our own eyes the stone bench where the Master had been lain. I walked in, touched the empty slab, and saw the linens nearby. My friend Mary suddenly laughed, a beautiful sound that echoed in the empty tomb. The tears that glittered in our eyes were joined with more joyful gasps, laughs, and disbelief.

We didn't yet understand, but we believed!

You might wonder at God's wisdom to have chosen women as the resurrection's first witnesses, those who aren't taken seriously in daily life or in a courtroom. Remember: God often chooses the world's unlikely people for special tasks. It's his way.

Yes, Jesus is alive! His promised resurrection makes clear that his death was undoubtedly no accident; rather, it stands out as the central chapter in the story of new life.

A Prayer for the Heart

Lord Jesus, those who have long known this story's ending can find it hard to feel the wonder we ought. I am thankful for the story of Mary Magdalene at the tomb, which makes the story so alive!

Jesus, your resurrection today brings the true hope of new life to all people, in all places, in all circumstances. Your Easter promise is that we will one day rise up from the dead and out of our own tombs. Amid all the compelling evidence to the contrary, this world is blooming with your resurrection life, the life that is more powerful than death. Yes, Lord, I believe! Help my unbelief.

Reflect

What heaviness of heart or burden might I bring to the risen Jesus? What do I want to receive from him today?

Peter Paul Reubens, *The Women at Christ's Empty Tomb*, 1640, Oil on Panel

A Word from Matthew (28:7-10)

"Then go quickly and tell his disciples, 'He has been raised from the dead and indeed he is going ahead of you to Galilee. There you will see him.' This is my message for you." So they left the tomb quickly with fear and great joy, and ran to tell his disciples. Suddenly Jesus met them and said, "Greetings!" And they came to him, took hold of his feet, and worshiped him. Then Jesus said to them, "Do not be afraid! Go and tell my brothers to go to Galilee; there they will see me."

Mary Magdalene Speaks

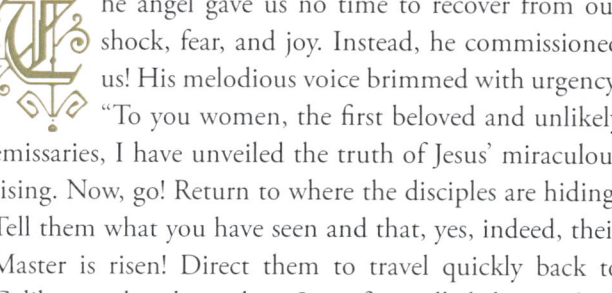

The angel gave us no time to recover from our shock, fear, and joy. Instead, he commissioned us! His melodious voice brimmed with urgency, "To you women, the first beloved and unlikely emissaries, I have unveiled the truth of Jesus' miraculous rising. Now, go! Return to where the disciples are hiding. Tell them what you have seen and that, yes, indeed, their Master is risen! Direct them to travel quickly back to Galilee, to the place where Jesus first called them, where they hold so many treasured memories. It is there Jesus will appear to them. Hurry, for there is no time to lose!"

Friends, when an angel with a face like lightning tells you to run, you run! But before we even passed through the cemetery gate, we heard a sound sweeter than music: His beloved voice, calling out his familiar greeting!

As his words reached my ears, a lump formed in my throat. Turning to see Jesus our Lord—whole, radiant, and not a drop of blood on his skin or clothing, filled my eyes with tears of joy. Without thinking, we all dropped to our knees and fell on our faces, worshiping him. Our trembling hands reached out and glided over his precious, still-pierced feet.

Our Master was not a mere mist or a hallucination. He was real! He was risen!

We kissed his hands. Tears streamed down our faces and stained the hem of his robe. Without realizing it, we were anointing the living Jesus, not the lifeless body we expected to find. Our hearts were full; our cups overflowed to an indescribable magnitude.

Only a few seconds passed before I again experienced holy fear as I sat before the angel. "How can I see the Son of God and—live?" The weight of Jesus' new glory kept my head bowed. None of us could look up; our eyes' longed to gaze on his beloved face.

Seeing easily into our hearts, Jesus offered us the exact words that the angel had spoken to us earlier, the same command God has so often given to our people: "Be not afraid."

My shoulders relaxed. I took a deep breath and looked up into Jesus' eyes. A holy rest and humble adoration filled every space in my heart.

After a few moments, Jesus left us. We hurried to the disciples, unable to contain our shouts of joy. The men were stunned by our news. They probably would not have taken us seriously without seeing the thrill and wonder on our faces. Obeying Jesus' directive, they left for Galilee immediately to seek their risen Master.

We would learn later that Jesus did go to Galilee, as the angel had declared, offering his bewildered disciples assurance, direction, forgiveness, and even some grilled fish for breakfast by the sea.

All this good news about Jesus and his appearance spread like a new wind ripple on a still lake. Only weeks later, thousands of Pentecost visitors in Jerusalem would hear Peter's preaching of the Good News. In the centuries ahead, millions of burdened believers would find an anchor of hope in our Master's message. Oh, how much easier it is to see now: The death of Jesus was no accident. He is risen! And even better, his story is far from over!

 ## A Prayer for the Heart

"Behold my servant will prosper…he will be high and lifted up and greatly exalted!" Father God, these prophetic words from Isaiah 52:13 finally came true that first Easter morning. Spirit, let me share in the amazement of the women who were the first witnesses of your empty tomb, and this scripture fulfilled. I believe you can use me, as you used those unlikely women, to share the Good News with my brothers and sisters and invite them to come, see, and worship the Risen Jesus. Help my unbelief.

Reflect

What part of Mary's surprising story would I most like to experience in this season of my life? Her great joy? Her encountering the risen Jesus, falling down to worship, and hearing his voice again? Her running to share this good news with the others?

James Tissot, *The Pharisees Conspire Together*, 1896, Watercolor and Graphite on Paper

A Word from Matthew (28:11-15)

While they were going, some of the guards went into the city and told the chief priests everything that had happened. After the priests had assembled with the elders, they devised a plan to give a large sum of money to the soldiers, telling them, "You must say, 'His disciples came by night and stole him away while we were asleep.' If this comes to the governor's ears, we will satisfy him and keep you out of trouble." So they took the money and did as they were directed. And this story is still told among the Jews to this day.

Nicodemus Speaks

I don't really know why I returned to my post on the Sanhedrin after Jesus' death. The priests' insufferable arrogance and bent toward manipulation nauseated me now more than ever. I suppose my return was partly out of habit but primarily out of fear—to cut ties with these men so soon after Jesus' death would have looked suspicious.

On the third day after Jesus' death, the temple guards who had been posted at Jesus' tomb burst into our council meeting, armor clanging and lungs gasping for air. Their faces, white with fear and shock, spoke their message before they even opened their mouths. Something had gone wrong. Very wrong. My mind began to race.

The leader among them told us Jesus' body was gone! He then described an earthquake, a glowing white being that had rolled away the stone to an empty tomb, and their complete and holy dread while paralyzed in the dirt. Two women, friends of the disciples, had seen everything and were just as overwhelmed as they had been. He was adamant that his men had not fallen asleep, or drunk too much wine, or been hallucinating. His account was sincere and could be trusted.

"This is impossible," some of my colleagues yelled. As for me, I longed to stand up, gird my robe, and run out of the chamber to see the tomb for myself. I didn't, though, fearing what they might do to me. Besides, I wanted to see what would transpire here amongst the Sanhedrin.

Caiaphas, his face red and the veins on his temples throbbing, cross-examined the guards repeatedly. They stuck to their story despite its incredibility. At this point, council members pointed out that their "rumors" could cause a commotion if allowed to leak to the crowds. If they failed to bury this Nazarene nonsense once and for all, the whole mess could end up being worse than before.

They planned to dismiss the guards' account as "false news" and then make up a more "believable" story to explain the empty tomb. They told the guards to spread the word that Jesus' disciples came at night and took away the body while the guards were fast asleep. Murmuring questions about the stone being too heavy for several strong fishermen to maneuver and the noise created upon trying to move it would awaken the soldiers were gaining traction in side conversations. These concerns were summarily overruled.

"Speak with authority," Caiaphas assured them, "and the masses will swallow the whole story, just as last Friday. And if the news of what happened does trickle up to Pilate, we will intervene and assure him—even if it takes a little bribe. And here, this should be enough to cover your promise to only tell our version of the story."

So the guards took his money pouch and pledged to never tell anyone else their original version of the story. Just as they had done with Judas, pieces of silver made rough places smooth.

I cringed. The irony of the situation was incredible. These priests had accused Jesus of deceiving the masses, and here they were doing the exact same thing. Didn't they know that God saw their duplicity? Noticing that others were not as angry as I was showed the difference between me and my Sanhedrin brothers. I was still struggling with sin and fear, but in Jesus' precious words, I was on the way to being born again.

The chief priests thought they were getting the last word on the situation by planting this false narrative about Jesus' missing body. But their lies could not withstand the groundswell of the true story told by the disciples and the women who had discovered the empty tomb first. Nothing would buy *their* silence. They had seen the risen Lord with their own eyes, and nothing that holiest of weeks had happened by accident.

❤ A Prayer for the Heart

Today's story shows me once again the contrast of truth and deception, of light and darkness. There are two storylines about what happened to Jesus on the cross and in the tomb. I must decide, whether for the first or the fortieth time, what I will believe about Jesus of Nazareth. How will I respond to what I have read and witnessed in Matthew's story? Will I commit to not only believing beyond logic but to also run and share the news with others?

Jesus, I believe I can speak the truth courageously and stand up strong in a world soaked in false narratives about you and your way here on earth. Help my unbelief.

Reflect

What stands out to me as I consider the religious leaders' relentless scheming and denial of the truth?

Szymon Czechowicz, *Resurrection*, 1758, Oil on Canvas

A Word from Matthew (28:16-20)

Now the eleven disciples went to Galilee, to the mountain to which Jesus had directed them. When they saw him, they worshiped him; but some doubted. And Jesus came and said to them, "All authority in heaven and on earth has been given to me. Go therefore and make disciples of all nations, baptizing them in the name of the Father and of the Son and of the Holy Spirit, and teaching them to obey everything that I have commanded you. And remember, I am with you always, to the end of the age."

Thomas the Disciple Speaks

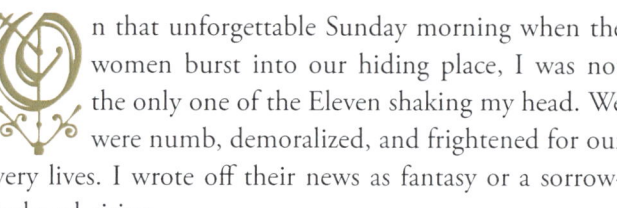

On that unforgettable Sunday morning when the women burst into our hiding place, I was not the only one of the Eleven shaking my head. We were numb, demoralized, and frightened for our very lives. I wrote off their news as fantasy or a sorrow-induced vision.

I was not alone in my skepticism of the women's claims. Peter and John's courage and curiosity made them follow the women to see if the story was true. Back quickly and out of breath, their news about the tomb helped us all to take the women's report more seriously.

Still stunned by the news and its incredible possibilities, we gathered our few possessions and prepared for the trip back to Galilee. I decided to go along; if something was true in all this commotion, I wanted to be there with my brothers. Besides, Galilee was far from Jerusalem and our Lord's persecutors. It seemed a good place to melt into the crowd and find temporary safety.

After arriving and settling in Galilee, we disciples took a walk up a favorite hillside. While enjoying the gentle breeze and sweet memories of being there with Jesus, we suddenly saw a familiar figure standing nearby. The blood rushed from my head, and I wondered: *Could this really be the Master?*

Some of us ran toward him like little kids, falling at his feet in awe and gladness. I'm not proud of it, but I held back. Not until I touched his hands and felt the wounds with my fingertips would my reluctant mind accept what my heart was hoping.

While we all alternated between doubt and delight, Jesus began speaking. "Because of my obedient death and the Father's eternal will, all authority now has been given me in heaven and on earth. You must leave your homes and go forth to all nations. Forget your assumptions about who belongs in my house and who doesn't, about who is clean and unclean. Include everyone.

"Follow the path I have shown you in my own ministry. Proclaim this good news in word and deed. Invite and then baptize everyone willing to hear to become part of my covenant family. Once they are grounded in knowing and doing all my teachings, send them out. They, too, are to help live out and lead others into this Great Commission.

"This is a vast and dangerous undertaking. You will be challenging the twin powers that rule over you, both the religious leaders who think they understand me and the caesars who rule as if they are gods.

"Don't be afraid. You will never be alone. All the resources of the Father, Son, and Spirit will be made available to you. Just as my Father was with Israel in the desert, I will be with you and in you. Always." He soon left us as mysteriously as he had appeared. I was left to ponder in my heart what had happened.

The following day, a seed of doubt threatened to choke the sprout of faith from the day before. *Were we just hoodwinked yesterday by a vision of our own making?*

Just a few days later, Jesus appeared to us again. Knowing me all too well, he singled me out and invited me to draw nearer. On his outstretched hands, I touched his wounds directly, which were now lingering scars.

After doing so, I could believe that Christ was my Lord and God!

What joy coursed through me as I spoke those words to my Master!

Over the next few days, Jesus continued to teach and encourage us, constantly reminding us that he couldn't stay here long. At first, with our hearts so fragile, we couldn't bear to see him go. He promised to send a helper, and at Pentecost, that promise was fulfilled. The Holy Spirit transformed us from a ragtag bunch of fragile disciples into apostles who would reach the nations.

That's a story unto itself!

With Holy Spirit leading the way, my tendency toward fear could paralyze me no longer. I started my ministry in Israel and eventually went to India to baptize and instruct new believers in Jesus' teachings.

We all soon came into conflict with earthly rulers, just as our Lord had predicted. Most of us who gathered on the mountain that day with Jesus would be later exiled, jailed, crucified, beheaded, or otherwise executed.

Similar fates awaited many of those who would later respond to the gospel. However, the path we were called to take was already worn smooth by the feet of our crucified and risen Savior.

His generous presence and faithful power expressed through us, his unlikely apostles, would forever remind the Church that Jesus' death and resurrection were no accident. They were the first fires and sure foundations of God's new and dramatic mission on earth.

❤ A Prayer for the Heart

Jesus, the disciples' combination of devotion and doubt, worship and weakness, is familiar territory for me. You know my heart well. Though I am not yet free of doubts and fear (I am, after all, human), you have given me your Spirit to unlock their paralyzing grip.

Thank you, Jesus, for inviting me to find myself in the crucifixion story and take my part in your unfolding story of redemption. Choosing as ambassadors those who disappointed, misunderstood, and doubted you make the Great Commission even greater. You are, and always have been, the hero of your story, the leader of the past, present, and future. So lead me. Lead us. And Lord, when doubt resurfaces, hold me close…and help my unbelief.

Reflect

This same commission from Jesus endures for every generation of his followers. How do I feel right now about my part in fulfilling this call to go and make disciples of all nations?

ROWN HIM WITH MANY CROWNS

THE LAMB UPON THE THRONE. HARK!

HOW THE HEAVENLY ANTHEM DROWNS

ALL MUSIC BUT IT'S OWN!

AWAKE, MY SOUL, AND SING

OF HIM WHO DIED FOR THEE.

AND HAIL HIM AS THY MATCHLESS KING

THRU ALL ETERNITY!

– MATTHEW BRIDGES (1800-1894)

www.ingramcontent.com/pod-product-compliance
Lightning Source LLC
Chambersburg PA
CBRC090838120626
46551CB00008B/694